DATE DUE

GAYLORD			PRINTED IN U.S.A.

The Hand of the Mighty

Also by the Author

Missions and Reconciliation (1969)
Faith at the Top (1973)
Memo for 1976: Some Political Options (1974)
The Spiritual Journey of Jimmy Carter (1978)
Land of Promise, Land of Strife: Israel at Forty (1988)
An Ethics of News: A Reporter's Search for Truth (1989)

The Hand of the Mighty

Right and Wrong Uses of Our Power

Wesley G. Pippert

Foreword by Paul B. Henry

BAKER BOOK HOUSE
Grand Rapids, Michigan 49516

Printed in the United States of America

Library of Congress Cataloging-in-Publication Data

Pippert, Wesley G., 1934-
    The hand of the mighty : right and wrong uses of our power /
Wesley G. Pippert.
        p.   cm.
    Includes bibliographical references and indexes.
    ISBN 0-8010-7115-1
    1. Power (Christian theology) 2. Service (Theology) 3. Watergate
Affair, 1972-1974. 4. United States—Politics and government—1977-1981.
I. Title.
BT738.25.Q56 1991
241'.62—dc20   91-6666
                                                                             CIP

Unless otherwise indicated, Scripture references are from the Revised
Standard Version. Other versions used are New Jerusalem Bible (NJB); King
James Version (KJV); New American Standard Version (NASV); New Revised
Standard Version (NRSV); New International Version (NIV).

To

David

my son

"Is not this David . . . of whom they sing and dance?"

—a proud father's paraphrase of 1 Samuel 21:11

Since then, there has never been
such a prophet in Israel as Moses,
the man whom Yahweh knew face to face.
What signs and wonders Yahweh caused him
to perform in Egypt against Pharaoh,
all his servants and his whole country!
How mighty the hand and great the fear
that Moses wielded
in the eyes of all Israel!

[Deut. 34:10–12 NJB]

God frustrates the devices of the crafty,
    so that their hands achieve no success.
He takes the wise in their own craftiness;
    and the schemes of the wily are brought to a quick end.
They meet with darkness in the daytime,
    and grope at noonday as in the night.
But he saves the needy from the sword of their mouth,
    from the hand of the mighty.

[Job 5:12–15 NRSV]

Contents

Foreword

I have had the privilege of counting Wes Pippert a close friend for almost thirty years. During those years we have argued over countless political questions. Sometimes we reached agreement. Other times we simply had to agree to continue disagreeing! But always I have benefited from the extraordinary range of experience that has shaped his perspectives on the great issues of the day. And always I have respected the manner in which he has struggled to integrate his deeply held Christian commitments with the contentious issues on which he daily reported to millions of Americans during his distinguished career.

For over three decades Wes Pippert has been a respected Washington political journalist. He has had access to the most politically powerful of the Washington insiders. He served as the principal UPI Washington correspondent during the Watergate crisis. He was White House correspondent for UPI during the Carter Administration. He served as senior Middle East correspondent for UPI from 1983-86. During both George McGovern's ill-fated campaign for the presidency and Jimmy Carter's successful campaign four years later, Wes Pippert was one of the "boys on the bus" who brought the excitement of the campaign trail to UPI-affiliated newspapers around the world. In addition, he has also had staff positions in the U.S. Senate and the U.S. House of Representatives.

But amid all the excitement of making the next deadline for tomorrow's early morning newspaper, Wes Pippert never lost sight of the fact that those who hold political power are supposed to be public "servants." In this book he explores the relationship between Christian servanthood and the exercise of political power. He examines not only the Watergate episode of the Nixon Administration but also the "little Watergates" of our private lives. And he readily admits that his own life—as well as yours and mine—has its own "little Watergates" of failed trust. His essay demonstrates the relationship between private morality and public morality, showing how the "least" of Christ's servants can in fact become an instrument through whom the mighty acts of God can be accomplished.

This book is not a cheerleader's guide to the simple "rights and wrongs" of the political system. It is, rather, a probing examination of the moralistic enthusiasm to which Christians and non-Christians often succumb in making their judgments on politics and political officials. We shall not all agree with all of the argument. But we will all benefit by having taken it to heart.

Paul B. Henry
Member of Congress

Preface

At the start of his ministry, the Gospels tell us, Jesus was tempted by the devil. Satan took him to a high mountain where his ultimate temptation was to offer Jesus the kingdoms of the world, an offer of consummate authority. Jesus turned him down.

Think of the implications of this story.

First, the devil, who is shrewd if nothing else, did not tempt Jesus with the lure of sex or the luxury of material goods. Rather, he tempted Jesus with what he thought that Jesus, if he was vulnerable to anything, might be vulnerable to: authority. He was tempting Jesus at the point of Jesus' strength. This temptation gives us a clue as to what might be the nature of *our* biggest temptation.

Second, the devil also saw the parallel between individual power and institutional power. Thus, he tempted Jesus, who was human as well as God, with personal glory intertwined with national grandeur. Too often we tend to separate individual power and institutional power, when actually both present similar perils to us. One tells us about the other.

I became fascinated by the exercise of power during my two-year assignment, from 1973 to 1975, as principal UPI Watergate reporter. I observed an arrogance of

11

power so blatant, a desire to propagate that power so intense, that a government almost fell.

A few years later, I was assigned to cover President Jimmy Carter. For all its problems, the Carter White House was an example of power used with restraint as well as in the pursuit of justice. Carter spoke of the president being "not First Boss but First Servant." He was the first American president in fifty years not to send troops into combat, and he refused to use force in trying to win release of the American hostages in Iran.

These two models—Watergate on the one hand, and the Carter White House on the other—drove me to the ancients. The study was riveting. What anchored me especially was my earlier graduate study in the Hebrew Bible.

This book is a study of the right and wrong uses of power.

"Power tends to corrupt; and absolute power corrupts absolutely," Lord Acton said.[1] But I believe he was wrong. I also differ with the esteemed Jacques Ellul and my good friends and colleagues, Cheryl Forbes and Anthony Campolo, Jr., who, I suggest, overly broad-brush *all* power as bad. Richard Foster comes closer to grasping the intrinsic paradox of power as something that can be used for good *or* ill.

My contention is that power per se is morally neutral; it is what we do with power that counts. It is also my contention that there is a remarkable parallel between corporate bodies and individual persons in this regard. Nations and individuals alike use power in similar ways; they are tempted by it in similar ways. Ellul saw that individual and institutional sin are closely related. "A major fact of our present civilization is that more and

---

1. Lord Acton, *Essays on Freedom and Power* (Boston: Beacon Press, 1948), 365.

more sin becomes collective, and the individual is forced to participate in collective sin."[2]

Michael Timmis, a noted Christian businessman, has said that he does not see any major distinction between the operations of Christian movements and secular ones. The evangelists Jim Bakker and Jimmy Swaggert remind us that even those who speak in the name of the Lord can fall victim to their own power. None of us is exempt. We all have power, even the most frail and self-effacing among us. And are not even the least of us tempted to use our personal power as force to have our own way, to impose our will on others, to control them? Do not even the least of us face our own Watergates?

There is hope for all—those who knowingly wield power, those who feel helpless and emasculated and powerless, those who are cynical—that they can become servants. The devil knew even before Jesus started his ministry that he would be the most powerful leader of all time—charismatic, courageous, visionary, inspiring, merciful, authoritative, serving—a powerful servant. We, too, can become powerful servants.

This book, the writing of which spanned eight years, examines power and its implications. Chapter 1 defines power and shows how all of us have it; chapter 2 discusses the abuse of power; chapter 3 examines the use of power as servanthood for the good of others; chapter 4 talks about exercising power as authentic leadership. In short, power used in the wrong way becomes force, violence, manipulation; but power used in the right way becomes service and care for others, and the pursuit of justice.

2. Jacques Ellul, *The Presence of the Kingdom*, trans. Olive Wyon, 1948 (New York: Seabury, 1967), p. 13.

Acknowledgments

I am indebted to many people for helping shape the insights and content of this book. Grant Dillman, former UPI Washington bureau chief, assigned me to the Watergate scandal and the Carter campaign and presidency, the two incidents that set my mind thinking about the use and abuse of power. Representative Paul B. Henry personifies ideally how power can be used to persue justice in a way that is both right and pragmatic. His office, in which I spent several months in 1989, embodies his ideals. Tom Getman, Steve Moore, Richard Pierard, Robert Clouse, Paul Michelson, Philip Loy, Sir Fred Catherwood, Os Guinness, and Mark Amstutz made helpful suggestions early on when my thoughts had not yet focused.

I thank Allan Fisher at Baker Book House, who was willing to gamble on my most controversial thesis—that individuals and nations can learn from each other about the exercise of power. Alice Freligh Macondray, Greta Rey, and Betty De Vries were three of the best editors ever to work on my words and ideas.

I especially am grateful to four men—Senate chaplain

15

Richard Halverson, Cal Thomas, James A. R. Johnson, and Dr. Gary Anderson—who provided guidance during the difficult days of the final drafts. Dr. Will Norton was also a bulwark. I can never repay their succor.

A host of others buttressed me as well: Dr. Edward W. Bauman, my pastor; Carlisle and Connie Dunaway, Dr. William Millard, and others at the Georgetown Discussion Group; Ken Daniel, Bev Godwin, and the others at the CBS Monday night group; Mary Wise and prayer partners; Drs. Harold Best, Mark Fackler, and Glenn Arnold; Andrew Burrows and Rick Hurst, my Jerusalem brothers; William B. and Dorothy Barton; Dr. Gordon Sabine and Dr. Jud Carlberg, my academic mentors; Wendy Geagan and Lee Grosscup; John Painter and Susan Reese; Dr. John and Nancy Gillespie; Clarke and Judy Brinckerhoff; John and Mary Finch; Dr. Donald Jones and Dr. Michael Ryan; and professional colleagues Nathaniel and Elizabeth Nash, Stan Cloud and Lynne Olson, Brooks and Bev Jackson, Bob and Sherry Andrews, Roy Howard and Shirley Beck, Ev and Jan Bauman, Melinda Gipson, Mike Cromartie, and Don Phillips.

I have been blessed with family. Rebecca, my wife. Paul, Marie, Harriet, and Harold, my brothers and sisters. My bevy of nephews and nieces, super-achievers all, but who never have lost their sweetness and sensitivity (the right use of power!). And Elizabeth and David, my children. Who could not fail to be sustained and inspired by their frequent, spontaneous remark, always accompanied with a massive hug, "I love you, Daddy."

1

What Is Power?

Ι once heard a sermon illustration about power that I've never forgotten. Power? the minister asked. He didn't mention the great armies of the world or the titans of industry and politics or the strength of an athlete. Rather, he asked us to think about the wildflower wedged in a tiny crack in a blacktop parking lot, a plant so fragile it could easily be pinched off, yet so strong it could push its way literally between a rock and a hard place.

We are like that little plant, although we may feel more like a straggly weed than a delicate flower. As individuals, all of us possess power perhaps in ways we don't realize. We can use that power to spread the fruit of either good or ill. We Americans are a people who are characterized as the most powerful on earth, a nation that has shown the most largesse of any country in the history of civilization but also a nation that has developed the most deadly weapons ever conceived.

Power. What is it? Where does it come from? How do we use it? What are its perils to avoid, its good to pursue?

Definitions of Power and Related Terms

Power is the ability to shape and influence people and/or events.

"The benefit of power," said Richard M. Nixon, "is that you can do something."[1] "Power," said Clark Clifford, aristocratic Washington lawyer and adviser to presidents since Harry S. Truman, "finally resolves itself into the equation of knowing how to accomplish the purpose that you set out to accomplish."[2]

Sociologist Dennis H. Wrong defines power this way: "Power is the capacity of some persons to produce intended and foreseen effects on others."[3]

"In short," writes political journalist Hedrick Smith, "the most vital ingredients of power are often the intangibles. Information and knowledge are power. Visibility is power. A sense of timing is power. Trust and integrity are power. Personal energy is power; so is self-confidence. Showmanship is power. Likability is power. Access to the inner sanctum is power. Obstruction and delay are power. Winning is power. Sometimes, the illusion of power is power."[4]

All of us hold power in awe; many of us covet it. We probably feel it is primarily the province of presidents and dictators and the rich. Governments and corporations have power. Governments can levy taxes and raise

1. NBC, *Today*, May 1, 1990.
2. Transcript, "The Power and the Glory," WETA, Washington, July 1982.
3. Dennis H. Wrong, *Power: Its Forms, Bases and Uses* (New York: Harper & Row, 1979), p. 21.
4. Hedrick Smith, *The Power Game: How Washington Works* (New York: Ballantine, 1988), p. 42.

armies; corporations can control the marketplace and manipulate the economy.

But we limit our view of what power is by thinking that only governments and corporations have it. An easy error is to think of power exclusively in terms of overt strength. The opposite often is true. Everyone has power. All of us have it in ways that we may not be aware of. Each of us, no matter how humble, exercises some form of power over the people within our circle of personal contact and, by way of such things as voting, buying, and opinion, on people beyond our physical spheres.

The parent obviously possesses tremendous power over the young child, a power that often persists through the entire lifetime of the parent and even beyond. On the other hand, the parent can, and frequently does, succumb to the manipulative power of a youngster bent on getting his or her way. The naughty boy seeking to impose his will on parents is little different from the Stalinist Soviet Union that imposed its will on Eastern Europe after World War II. Imposing of will is a matter of degree, ranging from childish manipulation to blatant bludgeoning of a people.

The verbal person often has tremendous persuasive power, either from the lectern or in one-to-one conversation. On the other hand, the reticent person sometimes can use silence or a few well-chosen words just as powerfully as the more loquacious person.

The servant often exerts power over the master or mistress. How? By catering to the creature-comfort needs the employers find important to their personal well-being. For instance, who has the real power at the moment a high-powered executive's high-priced auto breaks down on the freeway and a good-samaritan mechanic stops by to lend a hand?

We can abuse power in ways that are quite similar to the ways used by dictators and totalitarian governments.

When we look at our government we are not looking at a totally-other entity, we are looking at the collective extension of ourselves. Before we condemn the use of force by our government, for instance, we may ask ourselves how we are similarly abusing our abilities to impose our wills on others in ways that diminish them. Conversely, is there not a serious inconsistency when we are caring and kind in our personal lives but assert pride in a macho national government?

Authority is delegated power. In America, for instance, the people have self-governing power, but through the ballot box they delegate it to various authorities. A parent delegates power over the child to the nanny or the babysitter, and then to the educational system, from day care centers through graduate schools.

Force is power used as coercion. Force can be used appropriately to restrain evil. We accurately speak of a nation's "armed forces." Israel calls its army the Israel Defence Forces (IDF). The policeman often responds to situations with force. The parent who spanks the naughty child has resorted to force. The problem, as I shall point out later, is that force often degenerates into violence or manipulation.

Leadership is the effective use of power over others, generally groups of people. It is not to be confused with administrative or managerial skills or even official authority. Leadership transcends such authority and becomes something wholly apart. Leadership is the wielding of a unique kind of power. Leadership is the exercise of emotional and character traits that enable a person to marshal others, particularly collectively, to a cause. Like power, leadership is morally neutral. A leader is a visionary, able to attract and direct others. An effective leader can be a tyrant; an effective leader can also be benevolent. I say more about this in chapter 4.

The Source of Power

God, of course, is the ultimate source of power. (I devote the second part of this chapter, the case study, to the Bible's thorough discussion of power.)

As individuals we derive power from our talents and abilities. God's power is channeled to us as gifts from the Holy Spirit (Rom. 12; 1 Cor. 12). Clearly these gifts are distinctly spiritual in nature. But our individual talents and innate abilities, also, are created in us as gifts from God. We can choose to develop them as vocations or professions to support ourselves and our families; we can use them in serving God and our communities; we can use them for good or evil.

A talent may be the tremendous leaping ability of Michael Jordan or Mikhail Barishnikov, a power so awesome that when they leap they seem to hang suspended high in the air. A talent may be the shrewdness in talking that enables us to persuade others to our ways of thinking despite the moral superiority of their positions. A talent may simply be an uncanny ability to make even the most obstinate engine run, a talent that my brothers Paul and Harold have (and one that I covet).

Whatever our talents or abilities, they give us the potential of rising above others who are not as able as we are in those areas and to exercise power over them. And because we know that to be true, we open the way to making a huge error. Our special abilities give us an edge over others and a dark chance to overpower or take advantage of them.

Individuals do not exist in isolation nor always exercise power autonomously, however. People form groups; groups form communities; communities form nations. So, too, does ability and its resultant power become collective. In the arena of nations the people hold the power.

In the long run, governments rule only at the people's whim and willingness to be governed. (Ultimately, of course, governments rule only under God's sovereignty.) This is obvious in democracies. It is especially true in the parliamentary system, in which the prime minister is ousted from office upon losing the confidence of the legislators who elected the prime minister and of the people who elect the legislators. It is true even in the United States, where the president serves a fixed term no matter how much or how little support he has.

During the Watergate crisis, Richard Nixon lost the support of the people. A man once high in Nixon's administration (rumored by some to have been "Deep Throat," the still-unidentified source of many of reporters Bob Woodward and Carl Bernstein's revelations) told me how Nixon's administration had ground to a halt. The simplest decisions could not be made, even such relatively unimportant ones as getting approval on special-edition postage stamps. But Nixon remained in office until it became clear to him that he had irretrievably lost the support of the people. Then, and only then, did he resign.

Even in a dictatorship the people ultimately will reclaim power. This may not be apparent to the people who long have suffered under an oppressive and tyrannical government. But eventually the people will prevail. This was demonstrated in the winds of freedom that swept Eastern Europe and began to stir in China and South Africa as the decade of the 1990s arrived. No one could have predicted those events even a year earlier.

In an essay titled "The Power of the Powerless," written fifteen years before he helped topple communist rule in Czechoslovakia, playwright Vaclav Havel astutely analyzes why the people ultimately prevail.[5]

---

5. Vaclav Havel, "The Power of the Powerless," in *Living in Truth*, ed. Jan Vladislav (London: Faber and Faber, 1987), pp. 36–122.

Havel coins the term *post-totalitarian*[6] to refer to the Soviet control of Czechoslovakia. In a traditional dictatorship, a small group of people seize power and wield it over the majority. But the post-totalitarian system that Havel describes demands total and pervasive conformity, discipline, and a kind of blind automatism. By accepting post-totalitarianism, or at least tolerating it, the people, Havel said, "must *live within a lie*" (Havel's emphasis).[7]

Havel speaks of "the profound crisis of human identity brought on by living within a lie,"[8] whether of the identity of an individual or a society. The dissident, who may be simply a physicist, a worker, a poet, chooses to "live in the truth." Havel describes the dissident's task: "to trace the virus of truth as it slowly spreads through the tissue of lies, gradually causing it to disintegrate."[9] This "living within the truth" leads to an "inner emancipation"[10] from which emerges an "independent life of society"[11] alongside of but apart from the official, post-totalitarian structures. These dissident movements have an impact on society and the power structure not in systemic changes "but in a real, everyday struggle for a better life 'here and now.'"[12]

Havel uses the example of the manager of a fruit and vegetable shop who always, when told to do so, puts a slogan in his window among the carrots and onions: "Workers of the world, unite!" One day he decides not to put the slogan in the window merely to ingratiate himself. He decides not to vote in farce elections. He begins to say what he really thinks. Of course, he soon loses his shop and is transferred to another shop at less pay. But Havel describes what really has happened:

6. Ibid., 40.
7. Ibid., 45.
8. Ibid., 62.
9. Ibid., 60.
10. Ibid., 85.
11. Ibid., 86.
12. Ibid., 113.

By breaking the rules of the game, he has disrupted the game as such. He has exposed it as a mere game. He has shattered the world of appearances, the fundamental pillar of the system. He has upset the power structure by tearing apart what holds it together. He has demonstrated that living a lie is living a lie. He has broken through the exalted facade of the system and exposed the real, base foundations of power. He has said that the emperor is naked. And because the emperor is in fact naked, something extremely dangerous has happened: by his action, the green grocer has addressed the world. He has enabled everyone to peer behind the curtain. He has shown everyone it *is* possible to live within the truth.[13]

Thus, Havel says, "the most intrinsic and fundamental confrontation between human beings and the system takes place at a level incomparably more profound than that of traditional politics."[14] It is, he says, an "existential revolution."[15] But it is painful at the same time. "There are times when we must sink to the bottom of our misery to understand truth," Havel writes.[16] He would have to go to prison after he wrote those words before he would see the emancipation of Czechoslovakia.

Alexander Solzhenitsyn's power, Havel says, "does not reside in some exclusive political influence he possesses as an individual but in the experience of those millions of Gulag victims which he simply amplified and communicated to millions of other people of good will."[17]

While I was a foreign correspondent in the Middle East, an Israeli military commentator observed astutely that in any peasant war the people will always prevail, no matter how sophisticated and strong the tyrant's military

13. Ibid., 56.
14. Ibid., 114.
15. Ibid., 115.
16. Ibid., 89.
17. Ibid., 80.

force may be. The Americans saw it happen in Vietnam; the Israelis saw it happen in their 1982–85 occupation of southern Lebanon.

In centuries past, wars were "tidier," fought between nations. In the twentieth century, however, the people have often fought their governments. Eric Wolf has analyzed the peasant movements in the revolutions in Mexico, Russia, China, Vietnam, Algeria, and Cuba.[18]

Eighteenth-century British political philosophers David Hume and Edmund Burke examined the paradox of people power. They suggested that authority is a trust conferred by the people for their benefit. When rulers become so oppressive that government no longer affords the people security and protection, what Hume called "immediate sanction"—the people's obedience to the government—no longer remains in force.[19]

Elaborating on this, Burke, a conservative political philosopher, said: "Although government certainly is an institution of divine authority, yet its forms, and the persons who administer it, all originate from the people." He recognized the ultimate right of the people to rebel against oppressive government.[20] Oppression never endures to the bitter end; even oppressed people will reclaim the power that rightfully is theirs.

William Pitt the Elder before the American Revolution said: "The poorest man in his cottage may bid defiance to all the forces of the crown."

During the American Civil War military forces in Indiana convicted a civilian man who was a copperhead (a person sympathetic to the South) of treason and sen-

18. Eric Wolf, *Peasant Wars of the Twentieth Century* (New York: Harper & Row, 1969).

19. Robert S. Hill, "David Hume," in *History of Political Philosophy*, ed. Strauss and Cropsey (Chicago: Rand McNally, 1972), p. 526.

20. See discussion by Francis Canavan, S.J., ibid., pp. 659–679.

tenced him to death. The great jurist Jeremiah Black argued before the United States Supreme Court in *Ex parte Millikin*[21] that from the Magna Carta on down, the great documents of law had sought to preserve the liberties of the people. The Supreme Court agreed, rejecting the argument that President Lincoln had any inherent power to ignore or suspend any of the guarantees of the Constitution. Justice David Davis said, "The good and wise men who drafted and ratified the Constitution foresaw that troublous times would arise, when rulers and people would become restive under restraint and seek by sharp and decisive measures to accomplish ends deemed just and proper, and that the principles of the Constitution would be put in peril unless established by irrepealable law."[22]

The Danger of Power

Power is like money and sex. It's what you do with it that matters. This is the dilemma. Theologian Lewis Smedes has written: "Power itself is neutral. It can be harmful and destructive, or creative and helpful."[23]

Gentle persuasion can become subtle manipulation. Sex can be an act of love, but when done with force it becomes rape. Parental discipline used with excessive force becomes child abuse. Police authority used in excess becomes police brutality. The power-hungry pastor moves from being the spiritual shepherd of his flock to presuming to speak for God in governing every aspect of his congregation's life together. Since all of us can wield power

21. 4 Wallace 2, 121.

22. *Hearings Before the Select Committee on Presidential Campaign Activities, U.S. Senate, 93rd Congress* (Washington, D.C.: Government Printing Office, 1973), 6:2630–2631.

23. Lewis Smedes, *Love Within Limits* (Grand Rapids: Eerdmans, 1978), p. 12.

through our unique abilities, all of us are subject to the temptation of abusing power.

An individual can turn power into coercion and a determination to control others. And as the Nixon administration demonstrated, corporate or political power, even in America, can degenerate into a macho attitude, brute strength, and raw force. Dennis Wrong says the ultimate form of force is violence: direct assault on the body of another to inflict pain, injury, or death.[24] Wrong's insight fits institution and individual alike.

Jon Mintz, a reporter for the *Washington Post*, has made this succinct observation: "Washington is a city that worships power and title."[25] The question is, what does Washington do with that power?

Democratic politician Robert Strauss, one of the most affable and wily wielders of power in that city of power, said this in an interview:

Sometimes there's a lot of just smoke and mirrors to it and other times it's real; and power sounds like it's ruthless or cruel or sinful or something wrong with it. Power doesn't have to be those things, [but] it can be; that's when you abuse it. But power, also, is the ability to use the press, to reach the media; to change the course of events through relationships with people who have confidence in you; or you can go state your case and be heard and, if you're right, if you're persuasive, effect the course of an issue. That's power.[26]

In Shakespeare's *Measure for Measure* the nun Isabella remarks:

> O, it is excellent
> To have a giant's strength;

24. Wrong, *Power*, p. 21.
25. National Press Club luncheon, September 17, 1990.
26. "The Power and the Glory," WETA.

>   but it is tyrannous
>   To use it like a giant.[27]

I want to repeat the caution against contending that all power is all wrong. For if all power is wrong, then the power of the Holy Spirit, also, is wrong. And I want to guard against the error of saying that all use of force is wrong.

Jesus, however, was unambiguous. His directive is to prepare, negotiate, and avoid the use of force if possible.

> To him who strikes you on the cheek, offer the other also. [Luke 6:29; also see Matt. 5:39]

> When a strong man, fully armed, guards his own palace, his goods are in peace. [Luke 11:21; also see Matt. 12:29 and Mark 3:27]

> Or what king, going to encounter another king in war, will not sit down first and take counsel whether he is able with ten thousand to meet him who comes against him with twenty thousand? And if not, while the other is yet a great way off, he sends an embassy and asks terms of peace. [Luke 14:31-32]

There is precedent in the Hebrew Bible for both negotiation and preparedness. Moses negotiated with Pharaoh (Exod. 5–12). Jepthah negotiated with the Ammonites (Judg. 11:12). And King Jehoshaphat of Judah placed forces in the fortified cities of Judah, "and all the kingdoms of the lands that were round about Judah . . . made no war against Jehoshaphat" (2 Chron. 17:10).

Note the progression of Jesus' words above. He said, in effect, do not retaliate; be prepared, and try to negotiate. Jesus appears to suggest that these principles are as valid in interpersonal relationships as in the international arena.

27. Act 2, scene 2.

Many people in the world, including followers of God, never get past interpreting power as the wielding of force. But the biblical bases for this assumption are comparatively few. Much more frequently God uses his power in a just and merciful way.

Jacques Ellul has said that to argue that power in itself is indifferent—that it can be used for good or evil—is far too simplistic and all-encompassing. Rather, he contends that "all authority—psychic, charismatic, or functional— is necessarily linked with force, that is, with some constraint and repression. In the same way there is no such thing as objective, neutral power. All power is tied to the exercise of force and, therefore, to constraint, and sometimes to violence." Power runs wild, Ellul believes. There are values it cannot reach by the very nature of its reality: it necessarily implies the subordination of people. "There is no other way," he writes.[28]

But I believe there is.

Anthony Campolo, Jr., defines power as "the prerogative to determine what happens and the coercive force to make others yield to your wishes—*even against their own will*. This last phrase is crucial, for the coercive nature of power gives expression to its potential for evil. Coercion is the crux of why power is irreconcilable with Christianity."[29] Campolo is accurate in the first part of his definition of power. But Campolo's complete definition more accurately describes only the force or coercion—one aspect of power—that can degenerate into violence.

Cheryl Forbes falls victim to the same problem. She

28. Jacques Ellul, "Lust for Power," trans. by monks of New Skete, Cambridge, N.Y., *Katallagete: Journal of the Committee of Southern Churchmen* 7/2 (Fall 1979): 30–33.

29. Anthony Campolo, Jr., *The Power Delusion: A Serious Call to Consider Jesus' Approach to Power* (Wheaton: Victor, 1983), p. 11. The emphasis added is Campolo's.

writes "about power—what it is, what it means, how it seduces and sickens and eventually strangles those who think they control it, but who find in the end that it controls them."[30]

Richard J. Foster, I feel, comes closer to grasping the dilemma of power in his contrasting "destructive power" on the one hand with "creative power" and "the ministry of power" on the other.[31] Within this framework we can see that the powerful can become servants committed to others. Therefore, since all of us have power, all of us have the opportunity to use power in service to others, a concept we shall continue to develop throughout this book.

Thus, we see that all of us have power, from the least of us to the most mighty nation in the world. As we shall see in the following chapter, all of us are prone to abuse our power, whether we are faint of heart or mighty of hand.

30. Cheryl Forbes, *The Religion of Power* (Grand Rapids: Zondervan, 1983), p. 12.

31. Richard J. Foster, *Money, Sex & Power: The Challenge of the Disciplined Life* (San Francisco: Harper & Row, 1985), Part III, pp. 173–227.

Case Study
The Power of God

To repeat our assumptions: Power, the ability to shape or influence people or events, comes from God and in itself is morally neutral. Authority is power that either an individual or a group has delegated to someone else. Force is power or authority that is used coercively or manipulatively and can lead to violence.

The Bible has profound insights on power—what it is and how it ought to be used. An examination of the nuances and meanings of *power* in Scripture, particularly in Hebrew and Greek, can be distinctively enlightening.

The Hebrew Testament's understanding of power is much more subtle and complex than that of the New Testament. It uses several Hebrew words that have similar meaning: power, might, strength, force. These terms often are used interchangeably, and to draw a precise, distinctive meaning for each is impossible. It is no coincidence that the Hebrew Testament has many more references to power than the New Testament, which refers more frequently to authority. We conclude that God held power in the Hebrew Testament, but in the New Testament he delegated it to Jesus, who in turn delegated it to his followers.

In this study I am using the common, modern translations of these Hebrew words. The translations are provided by Joel Greenberg, whose combined command of Hebrew, English, and Arabic may be unmatched. He speaks all three daily. He is an American Jew who lives in

Israel, a Nieman Fellow journalist, son of a rabbi scholar, and former colleague of mine. I purposely use his common translations rather than the academic translations so that we can see and understand the Scripture in a modern way. I also use these common translations quite literally, sometimes at the expense of lucidity, to highlight the subtle distinctions the biblical writers may have wished to make when they used one word rather than another.

Hebrew Words for Power

כֹּח *koach*. This is the common word for power or strength. It is easily used by nearly everyone in modern Israel. We will translate usages of this Hebrew word "power."

גבורה *gvura* [Greenberg translation]. *geborah* [Harris-Archer-Waltke]. This word means strength or heroism. In modern Israel it has the connotation of bravery or courage. We will translate usages of this word as "heroic strength."

חַיִל *hayil*. This is a stilted or fancy word meaning "strength" or "power." It has physical connotations, and in modern Israel it also suggests success, as in "He's doing very well."

עֹז *oz* [Greenberg translation]. *az* [Harris-Archer-Waltke]. This word means courage or might. The Israeli army has an "oz" medal awarded for courage. We will translate this word as "courageous might."

For purposes of comparison, *The Theological Wordbook of the Old Testament*[1] uses the shorthand of equating the Hebrew כֹּח *koach* with power, the Hebrew גבורה *geborah* with might, and the Hebrew חַיִל *hayil* with physical strength or efficiency.

1. *The Theological Wordbook of the Old Testament*, ed. R. Laird Harris, Gleason L. Archer, and Bruce K. Waltke (Chicago: Moody Press, 1980).

English translations, unfortunately, often do great violence to our understanding of the biblical references to power. For instance, as we shall see, power resides in God. But English translations can carelessly attribute power to Satan, whereas the Greek or Hebrew word actually used is *authority*. Satan tempted Jesus at the start of his ministry by offering him authority over the nations, not power, as some English translations say (Luke 4:6). Even Satan knew he did not have power to give. One English translation speaks of "the power of Sheol" (Ps. 49:15), but the literal Hebrew translation refers to "the hand of Sheol." Christians struggle against worldly rulers of darkness (Eph. 6:12), but as we shall see, the Greek word for *power* is not used as a few English translations suggest.

Greek Words for Power

δυναμî *dunamis*. Power. Compare the English derivatives *dynamo* or *dynamite*.

εξουσια *ekousia*. Authority.

Jesus equates the Hebrew כֹּ *koach* with the Greek δυναμî *dunamis* by paraphrasing 1 Chronicles 29:11–12 in the Lord's prayer (Matt. 6:13 KJV); Paul also equates the same Hebrew and Greek words in Exodus 9:16 and Romans 9:17 RSV.

A survey of biblical references to power and authority reveal these truths about God as source and user of power. We will list the Hebrew and Greek roots only the first time the word appears. Throughout the chapter we will also translate the Hebrew *Yahweh* (יהוה) as LORD.

God as Source of Power, One of His Attributes

The power of God (δυναμî *dunamis*) exists from creation (Rom. 1:20) until the end of time (Rev. 19:1).

Almost from the beginning the LORD spoke of his power
(כֹּחַ *koach*) (Exod. 9:16), which Paul quoted (Rom. 9:17).
In his triumphant benediction, David said, "Thine, O
LORD, is the might, heroic strength (גְּבוּרָה *gvura*), glory,
victory, and majesty. . . . in thy hand are power and
heroic strength (1 Chron. 29:11–12). The psalmists frequently spoke of the power of God. David said courageous might (עֹז *oz*) belongs to God (Ps. 62:11). God rules
by his heroic strength forever (Ps. 66:7). The LORD shows
his people the power of his works (Ps. 111:6). David said
God used his power in creation (Ps. 65:6), which
Jeremiah also cites (10:12 and 32:17). A key purpose of
God's use of his heroic strength is to make his name
known (Jer. 16:21). Jesus said he will sit at the right hand
of power (Matt. 26:64; Mark 14:62; Luke 22:69).[2]

There is no authority (ἐξουσιά) except from God
(Rom. 13:1; Jude 25). Thrones, rulers, and authorities are
created through him (Col. 1:16).

God Uses His Power on Earth

God is in charge of history (Col. 1:15–20; Eph. 1:9–10).
Thus, he will prevail over evil, a reassurance we must not
forget in times of despair and setback. King Jehoshaphat
recognized that God used his power and heroic strength
to rule over all the nations (2 Chron. 20:6), sometimes to
help or sometimes to cast down, as a godly man told
King Amaziah when he hired some Israelite mercenaries
(2 Chron. 25:8).

Scripture's primary example of the LORD's using his
power in a forceful way was during the Exodus when the

2. These quotations are taken from my modern literal translations of the
Masoretic-Hebrew text as found in *The Interlinear Bible*, ed. and trans. Jay P.
Green, Sr. (Grand Rapids: Baker, 1976–79), and the 21st edition of Eberhard
Nestle's *Novum Testamentum Graece*.

Israelites fled from Pharaoh's army (Exod. 9:16 [which
Paul quoted in Rom. 9:17]; 15:6; 32:11; Num. 14:13;
Deut. 4:37). Psalm 106:8 refers to God's heroic strength
being shown in the Exodus. The LORD also threatened to
use his power to punish the arrogant and haughty king
of Assyria (Isa. 10:12–13).

Moses, in the one psalm of his we have on record, may
have been recalling Exodus when he spoke of the courageous might of God's anger (Ps. 90:11). The song of
Hannah, which Mary sang as her magnificat, declares
that people cannot prevail by their own power (1 Sam.
2:1–10). Indeed, the LORD can pull down the powerful
from their thrones (Luke 1:52). After the LORD put his
enemies to flight with wrath and fire, David praised the
LORD's courage and heroic strength (Ps. 21:13).

God Seldom Approves of Our Use of Force

It is a common fact that the oppressed often become
the oppressors. Just as the Egyptians used force to
make slaves of the Israelites (Exod. 1:14), so the liber-
ated Israelites subsequently used force in their new
land to enslave the Canaanites (Josh. 16:10; 17:13;
Judg. 1:28–35). After the kingdom was established,
Army Commander Joab put Adoram in charge of the
forced labor (2 Sam. 20:24). King Solomon used for-
eigners as forced labor (2 Chron. 8:8) and used them in
his vast construction projects (1 Kings 5:13–14; 9:15).
But even though they were enemies of Israel, the Lord
did not approve of crushing prisoners in this way and
depriving them of their rights (Lam. 3:34–36). Solomon
spared the Israelites from slavery (1 Kings 9:22). And
Paul admonishes masters to treat slaves justly and
fairly (Col. 4:1).

There was no aggression in Israel during a four-hundred-year period when charismatic judges ruled the relatively young nation. Only when Israel was threatened by a neighboring nation did it respond militarily. What foreign policy the judges had was defensive; they gained no new territory for Israel. Jephthah, who overcame a traumatic childhood to become an astute leader, used a round of negotiations in attempting to head off war with the Ammonites (Judg. 11:12). Scripture indicates Israel was much more under the direction of the Spirit of the Lord during the period of the judges than it frequently was during the warring years of the monarchy.[3]

When David took the throne he embarked on a series of wars to shore up Israel's boundaries, wars so bloody that God refused to let him build the temple. Solomon, on the other hand, apparently engaged in only one aggression, seizing Hamath-zobah (2 Chron. 8:3).

Force is not the ideal form of power, a lesson to be recalled during times of twentieth-century military buildups. A king is not saved by the size of his army, and a warrior is not delivered by great power (Ps. 33:16). The forceful do not retain their power, and heroic strength shall not save their lives (Amos 2:14).

Scripture seems to suggest that the power of God was used more frequently as a warning than in the actual exertion of force. Jesus said: "When a strong man, fully armed, guards his own palace, his goods are in peace; but when one stronger than he assails him and overcomes him, he takes away his armor in which he trusted and divides his spoil" (Luke. 11:21–22 RSV). This suggests that military preparedness can ward off aggressors.

In one intriguing use of the word, Luke says people are "forcing" their way into the kingdom of God (16:16).

---

3. Wesley G. Pippert, unpublished master's thesis, "The Politics of the Judges," Wheaton College, 1966, pp. 81–82, 93–94.

God Uses His Power Primarily for Justice, Righteousness, and Mercy

Repeatedly the biblical writers linked power and justice, or power and mercy, or braided all three together, strongly suggesting that one implies the others. In more than 120 representative chapters that mention justice, over half also speak of righteousness, often in the same sentence, and nearly twenty cite mercy. Thus, passages dealing with justice (Note: in this section I am using the term *legal justice* [שֹׁפֵט *shōpēt*].) and mercy help us understand how God defines power: It must be just and merciful.

Another concept on which the literal, modern rendering of the Hebrew text sheds great light is justice. Three Hebrew words have similar meanings:

מִשְׁפָּט *mishphat* and its related stem שָׁפַט *shophat* (to judge). These words in modern Hebrew have a legal implication. The referee in a soccer match is known as the מִשְׁפָּט. Therefore, we shall translate this word as "legal justice."

צָדַק *sadek* means to be righteous or just. In modern Hebrew, the word has religious implications.

יָשַׁר *ashar* literally means "straight" and in modern Hebrew is used to describe a person who is honest and has integrity. It has less of a religious and more of an ethical connotation.

The biblical insistence on justice, mercy, and righteousness is woven throughout the history of Israel and Judah. Mere power was not enough.

The Lord chose Abraham to become the father of a great nation and to keep the way of the Lord by doing legal justice and righteousness (Gen. 18:19). The Lord instructed the Israelites that in the Promised Land they should support the local judges and rulers who would govern with legal justice and righteousness (Deut. 16:18).

The Pentateuch was written at a time the Israelites were a rural people. Its concerns reflect justice to a people of the land. God told them to leave some gleanings in the field for the poor and the stranger (Lev. 19:9–10). Every seventh year, Moses said, set your slaves free (Exod. 21:2), a pattern that provided for the abolition of slavery (something the Western world did not achieve for more than 5,000 years).

Hannah pointed out that the LORD helps the poor, needy, and faithful, then observed acutely, "For not by power does a man find heroic strength" (1 Sam 2:9). Samuel's sons took bribes and perverted legal justice while serving as judges over Israel, deeds that led the elders of Israel to demand the establishment of a monarchy, which in effect rejected God (1 Sam. 8:1–7).

"Does God pervert legal justice? Or does the Almighty pervert the right?" Bildad asked plaintively (Job 8:3). Job's friends told him: "The Almighty we cannot find him; he is great in power and legal justice" (Job 37:23). Job declared that God would use his power to heed him, not contend with him (Job 23:6).

David linked mercy and the courageous might and the heroic strength of God (Ps. 21:7, 13). He linked mercy and courageous might when Saul was trying to kill him (Ps. 59:16 and Ps. 62:11–12). David said that the LORD is merciful and will work legal justice and right for *all* who are oppressed (Ps. 103:6–8). As king, David administered legal justice and righteousness to all his people (2 Sam. 8:15; 1 Chron. 18:14).

Psalms not necessarily written by David contain the same message. The wicked will not stand in legal justice or sinners among the righteous (Ps. 1:5). The LORD, lover of justice, will judge the world in justice, righteousness, and ethical integrity (ישר) *[ashar]* (Ps. 98:9; 99:4). He blesses those who observe legal justice and righteousness (Ps. 106:3).

King Solomon asked God that he might rule with legal justice and righteousness (Ps. 72:2), and the queen of Sheba observed that the LORD God put Solomon on the throne to do just that (1 Kings 10:9; 2 Chron. 9:8). Solomon said that a wicked man accepts a bribe and perverts legal justice (Prov. 17:23) and that knowledge and wisdom are stronger than power (Prov. 24:5).

The prophets wrote during a time Israel had become more urbanized, and they confirm the legal dimensions of God's notion of justice. Ezekiel condemned Sodom because its people had a glut of food and did not feed the poor (Ezek. 16:49). Malachi seemed to equate oppressing the wage earner with adultery and perjury (3:5). How are wage earners oppressed in our day? They may be deprived of a chance to work (unemployment) or their wages are chipped away (inflation). God is concerned about the nation's unemployment and inflation, and anyone who professes to follow him must be as well.

The LORD is exalted in legal justice and righteousness (Isa. 5:16). In the passage (Matt. 12:18–21) Jesus quoted, he will not fail or be discouraged until he has established legal justice on the earth (Isa. 42:1–4). Two eloquent passages sum it up: "Happy is he whose help is the God of Jacob, . . . who executes legal justice for the oppressed; who gives food to the hungry," (Ps. 146:5, 7). "Cease to do evil, learn to do good; seek legal justice, correct oppression; defend the fatherless, plead for the widow" (Isa. 1:16–17).

> I am the LORD, I have called you in righteousness,
> I have taken you by the hand and kept you;
> I have given you as a covenant to the people,

A light to the nations,
To open the eyes that are blind,
To bring out the prisoners from the dungeon,
From the prison those who sit in darkness.

[Isa. 42:6–7]

Even as the sun began to set on the kingdoms of Israel
and Judah, and the Israelites went into exile, the
prophets persisted in this theme of justice, mercy, and
righteousness. They said that the LORD shows forth his
legal justice every morning (Zeph. 3:5) and that he lives
in truth, justice, and righteousness (Jer. 4:2).

Ezekiel spoke bluntly to those who rule with harshness
rather than mercy: "Ho, shepherds of Israel who have
been feeding yourselves! Should not the shepherds feed
the sheep? You eat the fat, you clothe yourselves with the
wool, you slaughter the fatlings; but you do not feed the
sheep. The weak you have not strengthened, the sick you
have not healed, . . . the lost you have not sought, and
with force and harshness you have ruled them"
(34:2b–4). God told the princes of Israel to put away violence and oppression and to execute legal justice and
righteousness (45:9).

God Often Assigns Authority,
but Seldom Power, to Others

God delegates his power and authority. Thus, all
earthly powers and authorities are subject to God (1 Cor.
15:24).

The biblical references to *power* residing in the hands
of people are few, mainly limited to the following: King
Melchizedek of Salem (Gen. 14:18–20) had the power of
an indestructible life (Heb. 7:16). God gives courageous
might to his people (Ps. 68:35). Daniel said the power of

a great king would cause great destruction in the end times (8:24). Micah declared with confidence that he was filled with power, legal justice, and strength (3:8). The eunuch serving Queen Candace of Ethiopia had power (Acts 8:27), perhaps that of the servant.

Some atypical uses of *power* occur in the Hebrew Testament. Reuben, eldest of the twelve sons of Israel, was his father Jacob's power and might (Gen. 49:3). One manifestation of Judge Samson's power was his hair (Judg. 16). Saul got power from food (1 Sam. 28:20, 22), as did Elijah (1 Kings 19:6, 8).

However, God gave authority to people to rule over all other life on earth (Gen. 1:26). The Bible never speaks of the devil having power, only whatever authority[4] God permitted him to have. When Satan tempted Jesus at the start of his ministry, he offered him authority over the nations (Luke 4:6). In relating his conversion experience, Paul tells of turning from the authority of Satan to God (Acts 26:18).

The Bible recognizes that both morally good and bad persons can wield authority. When authority is attributed to someone other than Jesus or his followers, it generally is civil in nature (Rom. 13:1). The centurion whose slave was ill was under authority (Matt. 8:9; Luke 7:8). Pilate told Jesus he had authority to crucify or release him (John 19:10). Jesus referred pointedly to the "great men" of the nations who have authority over people (Matt. 20:25; Mark 10:42; Luke 22:25), and went on to say that those who would be first must be servants. Paul said that Christians struggle against authorities (Eph. 6:12) but also are to be submissive to them (Titus 3:1). The Lord gives believers the authority to build themselves up (2 Cor. 10:8). Before his

---

4. In the following sections, the Greek word for authority (ε'ξουσία) is always used in the text.

conversion Paul apparently was given authority by the chief priests (Acts 9:14; 26:10, 12) to prosecute Christians.

God Gave Authority to Jesus

God presented to Jesus authority over all things (John 5:27; 17:2; Col. 2:10; Rev. 12:10). Jesus acknowledged that the Father had granted him authority to judge (John 5:27). Jesus claimed authority over his life and said that authority came from God (John 10:18). Jesus asserted this authority by claiming it (Matt. 28:18; Luke 20:8). Jesus had authority to teach (Matt. 7:29; Mark 1:22). He had authority to forgive sins (Matt. 9:6; Mark 2:10; Luke 5:24). He had authority over unclean spirits (Mark 1:27; Luke 4:36), and Luke notes that Jesus had authority as well as power (δύναμις) over them. God gave Jesus authority to judge (John 5:27). The people recognized his authority (Luke 4:36). Even his opponents, the priests and elders, implicitly recognized this authority (Matt. 21:23; Mark 11:28–29; Luke 20:2). All powers and authorities were subject to him (1 Peter 3:22).

Jesus used his authority to be merciful. He healed the centurion's slave (Luke 7:1–10). He raised the widow's son from the dead (Luke 7:11–17). He fed the five thousand and the four thousand. The list of caring incidents, which dominated the first portion of his ministry, goes on and on. He began his ministry by saying he had come to aid the poor, the captives, the blind and the oppressed (Luke 4:18–19); he concluded it by saying those who did not feed the hungry and did not visit the sick and imprisoned would not inherit eternal life (Matt. 25:31–46). He condemned the Pharisees, the fundamentalists of his day, because they "neglected . . . justice and mercy" (Matt. 23:23; Luke 11:42). Christ's throne will be built on justice and righteousness (Jer. 23:5; 33:15; Isa. 9:7). Jesus quoted Isaiah 42:1–4 in saying he would proclaim legal justice to the nations (Matt. 12:17–21).

Jesus Gave Authority to His Followers

Christ, as head of all authority (Col. 2:10), granted authority to his twelve disciples (Matt. 10:1; Mark 3:14–15). Luke the physician adds that he also gave them power to heal (Luke 9:2). Jesus gave his seventy followers authority over snakes and scorpions and, significantly, to overcome the power of the enemy (Luke 10:19). Note the juxtaposition of power and authority. Paul suggests that the Lord gave all of his followers authority for edification (2 Cor. 10:8).

Then, something remarkable happened.

At Pentecost Jesus' Followers Received Power

After the resurrection, Jesus' power, not his authority, was recognized in his words and deeds. So, after Pentecost, Peter spoke of Jesus' powerful deeds (Acts 2:22). English translations refer to "miracles" (KJV) or "mighty works" (RSV) but the Greek text uses "powerful." Another unusual switch occurred. Luke records in Acts 1 that the coming of the Holy Spirit at Pentecost had been Jesus' promise of God's authority to grant the believers power (1:7–8). Paul says the gospel came in power (1 Thess. 1:5). The power that once was God's alone now belonged to Christ's followers.

John quotes a voice from heaven that says the power of God and the authority of Christ have come (Rev. 12:10). Paul declares that Jesus and his message are made up of the power of God (1 Cor. 1:24; Rom. 1:16).

We Ought to Use Our Power to Be Merciful

The strong implication is that we should use our power to be merciful. The apostle Paul says we must exert ourselves to help the weak (Acts 20:35). The signs of an apostle included powerful deeds (2 Cor. 12:12), and indeed, the Macedonian churches, although extremely poor, gave "beyond their power" (2 Cor. 8:3). In one translation of 2 Corinthians 8:14 (RSV), Paul says, "As a matter of equality, your abundance should supply their want," a strong suggestion for redistribution of wealth. James warns, "For judgment without mercy will be shown to anyone who has not been merciful. Mercy triumphs over judgment" (2:13 NIV).

$$2$$

The Abuse of Power

Personal Power

We are much more used to talking about the abuse of power at the political level than at the personal level. But the abuse of power is the same at both levels: it can be just as violent, just as manipulative, just as macho. One helps us understand the other.

An individual is entitled to have autonomy; so is a nation. But a person ought never to use that autonomy as an excuse for aggressively assaulting another person verbally, emotionally, physically; neither should a nation.

I want to examine how our talents and skills—our personal power—degenerate into attempts to control and manipulate, which are the personal equivalents of institutional or national force and violence.

Our Power Can Be Our Greatest Weakness

This is the surprising paradox: We are more likely to succumb to power's disease in our strength than in our weakness. Our greatest vulnerability to moral failure lies not in our weakness but in the area of our strength. Our greatest temptations occur in our talents and skills—our personal power—and not in our inadequacies and insufficiencies.

To use an ordinary example, as a boy I dreamed of being center fielder for the New York Yankees. I had a weakness, however. I couldn't catch anything hit in my direction. So trying to become a center fielder in the tradition of Joe DiMaggio and Mickey Mantle was never a lure. Those who are acquainted with me know that I can never be tempted to try to become a concert pianist, even though I would love to play the piano. My weaknesses had little relation to my temptations.

But I am vulnerable in other areas. We Pipperts are passionate, persistent people. We don't give up. Once committed to something I, as a Pippert, don't back off easily. That's a good trait often, but not always. As a result, I signed up for courses during my university days that I should have dropped but which I did not because I was so persistent. I worked for the same corporation for nearly thirty years, when I might have quit to pursue other jobs in the media. I have hung on to things that should have been excised from my life.

Let's look at other examples of temptations in strength, of how power mounts into force.

The power of verbal skills scarcely needs mentioning. From the time we were young when we sassed our parents, when we made cruel remarks to our schoolmates or were cut down by theirs—perhaps with lasting emotional scars—to our verbal control of our spouses, children, and fellow workers, or theirs of us, we have had a lifetime of coping with the temptations of word power. The Book of Proverbs devotes more than a hundred verses to our tongue, mouth, and words. Few other subjects are mentioned as frequently.

The power of intellectual prowess can degenerate into arrogance that is used to humiliate less quick-witted persons. Or, it can become a tendency to over-intellectualize, thus diminishing the emotional or spiritual content of a matter.

The downtrodden in their own way can be controlling. A common large-city experience is being humiliated when a beggar or homeless person seeking a handout shouts an epithet.

Children often use the power of their weakness to manipulate and control their parents. Children can fuss so much that parents, in despair, simply throw up their hands and let the children have their way.

Police officers continually have to be trained not to be too quick to use the force of their guns and billy clubs but to use nonconfrontational tactics first, which usually succeed.

Sales persons and advertisers use their powers of persuasion to foist unneeded products or services on the gullible. (And aren't most of us gullible about something?)

The abuse of personal power is not limited to these examples, of course. All of us are prone to abusing our power, as a little introspection will show. Let's now look at an explanation of why abuses of our personal power occur and at some detailed examples of how they take place.

How We Begin to Abuse Our Personal Power

The White House press corps travels in style. During my presidential watch I loved the trappings; oh, how I did! We traveled in chartered airliners with first-class configuration throughout the cabins, and all the food and drinks we wanted were served on white linen tablecloths. (Traveling with the president on Air Force One, which I did many times as a member of the press pool, wasn't nearly as much fun nor as lavish.)

The White House's travel office chartered the flights and reserved blocs of rooms at first-class hotels with pre-arranged check-in. A bus was always waiting on the tarmac to take us where we were going and to return us to the plane after the presidential event. Pretty soon it became very easy to feel that this kind of lavish treatment was our due, and woe be to anyone who fouled up things. One well-known colleague discovered at a hotel in Tokyo that his baggage had been misplaced, and he shouted at the Japanese desk clerk, "You deserved what we did at Hiroshima!"

I'm sure I succumbed as well to the seduction of those power trips, but at the same time I never could forget the model of my father, a giant of a man in more ways than one but humble, to whom pretense was a worse crime than thievery. I don't think I ever was on Air Force One without thinking about my dad.

As we grow to adulthood, we discover our talents and skills. We hone them through education and practice. Or we obtain personal power or access to power through our jobs, as I did as a White House correspondent and later as a foreign correspondent. Our intentions may be honorable—to serve others, to serve the kingdom of God. We are grateful for our abilities. We are proud of our accomplishments. We feel God is blessing us. At that point, probably unwittingly, we start to become vulnerable to temptation. We gradually grow to rely on our abilities as the source of our satisfaction. We grow more proud. We get used to the acclaim that our skills arouse in others, and we even start to think we are entitled to that acclaim. We believe we are above criticism, particularly in the areas of our talents. After all, we think, aren't these talents from God? Are they not stirring others? So what is there to criticize? Subconsciously we begin to believe that we, not God, are the source of our abilities and accomplishments. Subtly and even unintentionally we begin to use our power for selfish purposes. The outward expression of our talents becomes more important than our inner characters. We fall in love, not with ourselves but with the expression of our talents.

This erosion progresses in microsegments. We get by with a few small misdemeanors, minor by anyone's account. Then we get bolder in using our skills for our own purposes. Soon we begin using them to control and manipulate others, not to serve them.

Michael Timmis has observed that power and pride are indistinguishable. "Whenever you have an abuse of power," he once remarked to me, "you have pride." So there are the clear clues that can reveal to us when we are starting to abuse our power—a bit too much pride here, a bit of an inclination to cut corners, to take advantage of others, and finally, a desire to cling to our power at all costs.

The Bible says the exercise of our gifts and skills ought to enhance the community (1 Cor. 12:25–26). But when we start abusing our personal power, the exact opposite takes place: We enhance ourselves at the expense of others. Gradually inching toward using our power for self-centered purposes, each step seems to be the appropriate next move. All the while we rationalize what we do in altruistic and spiritual terms or childlike innocence.

Most Christians are at least as vulnerable, and possibly more so, to these temptations as the people we label pagans, and for very good reason. Politicians generally have a clear sense of why they want power; so do corporate titans. They know what they want and they know how to get it. There is little false modesty. But we Christians know our talents and abilities come from God. We easily may become convinced we are using them for his kingdom, and we may become blinded to the hard truth that our excess in using our talents and abilities is manipulative of others and therefore downright wrong. We seek to justify everything we do as "doing it for the Lord." Worst of all, we may not be aware of what we are doing.

While I was covering Watergate, which is the case study in the second half of this chapter, I rarely encountered any remorse among the defendants. They may have denied what they had done and may not have known why they did it, but they did not try to apologize. A few years later I happened to attend the backstage prayer meeting before a big religious meeting. One speaker after another prayed, "Oh, Lord, anoint my tongue with fire when I speak tonight! Speak through me! May I move these people!" Not one prayer was offered that said humbly and simply, "Lord, work in the hearts and minds of the people in the audience. That's all I ask." The speakers clearly forgot what the apostle Paul said of how others responded to him: "His bodily presence is weak, and his speech of no account" (2 Cor. 10:10). In these two situations, where was the greater honesty? Where was the greater deception?

A few years ago I interviewed Charles Colson, Watergate long behind him and by then an esteemed evangelical leader. Colson's fame is now far greater than it ever was. I asked him if the acclaim of the evangelical community he hears so frequently may be even more seductive than the behind-the-scenes power he held as White House special counsel. He seemed somewhat taken aback. "I may be deluding myself," he replied, not answering the question directly. "But I find it almost distasteful. I really don't like it. I find it's exalting man instead of Christ."

I once interviewed Carlisle Floyd about his 1981 musical drama, *Willie Stark*, based on the life of Huey Long. Floyd pointed out that even people who wish to do good can abuse power. Willie Stark (the German word for strong is *stark*) was a man who had convinced himself that he had a rare but genuine feeling for the plight of people, the dispossessed of the world.

"Therefore," Floyd said, "Willie Stark justifies anything he needs to do to protect the people's interests, never completely recognizing the personal element, which is also a need for a vindictive triumph over the professional power that humiliated him early in his career. So, ruthlessly and needlessly existing side by side is this rage, this exertion of power with a very genuine compassion for people."

In Floyd's drama, Willie Stark ponders: "Sometimes to do good a man has to sell his soul—I wonder, I wonder." So Willie Stark is left, in Floyd's words, "a very divided man," a portrayal that bears a striking resemblance to the apostle Paul's description of the inner war of sin: "when I want to do right, evil lies close at hand" (Rom. 7:21).

We must always be alert to what we do well, remembering that it can lead us to crisis.

To carry this paradox further, we are especially vulnerable when we are attacked at our point of strength. Why? When we are attacked at our point of weakness, our self-esteem is not bruised since we already are aware of that weakness; when we are attacked at our point of strength, we are being attacked where we are most confident, and we lose a measure of self-confidence and self-esteem. The emotional trauma can be devastating.

I became a father at age fifty, and to my great joy discovered that I loved being a father and even had some innate parenting skills. Later, someone criticized my parenting. It devastated me. If this person had said, "You're a lousy investigative reporter," it would not have hurt half as much. For although I have versatile skills as a reporter, I know that being a tough investigator is not one of them. But I love being a father, and when that talent was called into question, I felt like I was being knifed.

Using Our Talents to Control Others

Camus was an existentialist writer, often despairing—but accurate—in his view of human nature. In his book *The Fall*, the lawyer said his true desire was "not to be the most intelligent or most generous creature on earth, but only to beat anyone I wanted, to be the stronger, in short, and in the most elementary way. The truth is every intelligent man, as you know, dreams of being a gangster and of ruling over society by force alone."[1]

Power, thus, can be like a cancer—cells multiplying without regard. It can seek to perpetuate itself at any cost, such as the case study on Watergate reveals. It can undermine the trust of people in their superiors, as polls have told us about the diminishing trust of Americans in their institutions. It can seduce lesser lights; for example, notice the way the men of Watergate succumbed to its lure.

The power of persuasion, when used for good, is perhaps the king of all skills. But when the power of persuasion is used to communicate falsehood, terrible harm and hurt can result. On the political level, we call the person who uses the power of persuasion for the wrong purposes a demagogue. On the private level, we call the person who uses the power of persuasion for wrong purposes a con artist. Huey Long, Jim Bakker, and our companions who can talk us into anything share a common, dark theme.

This is actually seduction in the broader sense, but there is a literal truth in the contention that personal power is often used in a sexually exploitive way. It was not the personal appeal of Gary Hart and Congressman Wilbur Mills and a host of other disgraced public figures that led to their sexual affairs. It was their position of

1. Albert Camus, *The Fall*, trans. Justin O'Brien (New York: Knopf, 1956), p. 55.

political power. Power, as often is said, is the ultimate aphrodisiac; thus, power that is corrupted can lead to sexual sin. This is understandable.

For instance, why are pastors and psychologists vulnerable to having affairs? Part of it is that in their professional relationships they generally operate as the superiors, the ones with power, while the parishioners or the patients are the subordinates. But mostly, I believe, it is because they are in the business of being comforters, and they are good at it; that is their power. Put someone who gets little emotional support from his or her spouse into the care of a professional comforter, and you have the seeds of tremendous temptation and resultant trauma. The needy person responds to the gentle attention of the pastor or psychologist. Regretfully, pastors and psychologists may take advantage of such a situation.

Another too frequent example: Many devout Christians have distorted the biblical teaching about "headship" in the home into a sort of male tyranny that ignores the broader biblical teaching that all of us, men and women alike, are to serve one another (Eph. 5:21).

Some pastors, especially in fundamentalist or independent churches, use deception and delusion in their handling of Scripture to wield near dictatorial control over their congregations and members. They use self-asserted divine mandates to maintain this control. One clue to such situations is the way the pastors' names are emblazoned in huge letters on Sunday bulletins, in church advertisements on the religion pages of newspapers, or on signs outside their sanctuaries. These are not subtle assertions of their power. By contrast, my own pastor, Edward W. Bauman, is widely recognized as one of the nation's foremost pulpiteers; yet his name appears in the Sunday bulletin in small print no larger than, and along with, the rest of the staff's, including the other ministers, receptionists, secretaries, and custodians. To me that small print is another sign of his godliness.

Akin to this is the danger of cultism in conservative Christianity. A cult results when a good idea in its excess is distorted into something terrible and is imposed on others. Then the complex becomes simple; everything is clear-cut. The cult leader can diagnose a problem in moments and solve it almost as quickly. Never mind that most people do not perceive things the same way; the tiny band of the cult are confident they have a clear fix on reality.

Vaclav Havel, the Czech playwright who became president of his homeland, described the process eloquently: "This ideology inevitably has a certain hypnotic charm. To wandering humankind it offers an immediately available home: all one has to do is accept it, and suddenly everything becomes clear once more, life takes on new meaning, and all mysteries, unanswered questions, anxiety, and loneliness vanish. Of course, one pays dearly for this low-rent home: the price is abdication of one's own reason, conscience, and responsibility."[2]

Yale scholar Irving Janis has offered solid suggestions for preventing what he calls "groupthink," a phenomenon similar to cultism. Janis suggests that members of a group give high priority to the airing of individuals' objections and doubts; members of the group should discuss its deliberations with trusted associates; experts who are not members of the group should be invited on a staggered basis; one member should always be assigned the role of devil's advocate; and they should continually survey the warning signals from rivals.[3]

    2. Vaclav Havel, "The Power of the Powerless," in *Living in Truth*, ed. Jan Vladislav (London: Faber and Faber, 1987), 39. The essay was written in 1975.
    3. Irving L. Janis, *Victims of Groupthink* (Boston: Houghton Mifflin, 1972).

The prophet Ezekiel tells us what the Lord has to say to the cult-type leader:

> Because your heart is proud,
>   and you have said, 'I am a god,
> I sit in the seat of the gods,
>   in the heart of the seas,'
> yet you are but a man, and no god,
>   though you consider yourself as wise as a god—
> you are indeed wiser than Daniel;
>   no secret is hidden from you;
> by your wisdom and your understanding
>   you have gotten wealth for yourself,
> and have gathered gold and silver into your treasuries;
> by your great wisdom in trade
>   you have increased your wealth,
>   and your heart has become proud in your wealth—
> Therefore thus says the Lord GOD:
> Because you consider yourself as wise as a god,
> therefore, behold, I will bring strangers upon you,
>   the most terrible of the nations;
> and they shall draw their swords
>   against the beauty of your wisdom
>   and defile your splendor.
> They shall thrust you down into the Pit,
>   and you shall die the death of the slain
>   in the heart of the seas.
> Will you still say, 'I am a god,'
>   in the presence of those who slay you,
> though you are but a man, and no god,
>   in the hands of those who wound you?
> You shall die the death of the uncircumcised
>   by the hand of the foreigners;
>   for I have spoken, says the Lord GOD.
>
>   [Ezek. 28:2–10]

The Televangelists

The fallen televangelists are a classic example of the broader seduction that occurs through deception and delusion. (I make it clear here that I am not speaking of all televangelists, only those who have publicly and blatantly erred.)

The fallen televangelists did not leap from humble lifestyles to lavishness. They were both seduced and seducers. They were not mere country hicks. They were intelligent, highly effective communicators. Yet their very success and their illusions of invincibility insulated them from their vulnerabilities and from anyone who would talk straight to them. Their falling was not a reflection on the gospel they espoused but on their abuse of their talents and spiritual gifts. Success blinded the televangelists to their humanity. Their success seduced them.

Can anyone who heard Jimmy Swaggart's high-octane sermons wonder why he had problems controlling his passion in other areas? Jimmy Swaggart himself may have come closest to analyzing correctly what happened. "Why?" he asked. "I have asked myself that ten thousand times through ten thousand tears. Maybe Jimmy Swaggart has tried to live his entire life as though he was not human. . . . This gospel is flawless, even though it is ministered by flawed men."

The era of the televangelists did not begin this way. It was born a generation ago, not long after television itself. The TV preachers seemed to have a glimpse of something great: how to spread the Word to the four corners of the earth in our time.

Pat Robertson, a blue-blood Virginian, found the Holy Spirit and an abandoned TV station, and combined the two to form what is now the Christian Broadcasting Network. One of his sidekicks, Jim Bakker, and his wife, Tammy, split off and founded PTL. Swaggart was from

Louisiana, and in one sermon he boasted how he and his cousin, Jerry Lee Lewis, founded rock music; but Jimmy said he walked away from it because he felt it was evil. Robert Schuller was an Iowa farm boy who went to California, founded a church in an outdoor movie theater, and now has the Crystal Cathedral. Jerry Falwell stayed home in Lynchburg, Virginia, and founded Thomas Street Baptist Church. Rex Humbard was the son of an itinerant evangelist and went on to build the Cathedral of Tomorrow in Akron, Ohio.

Swaggart, Roberts, and Humbard were staked in the culture of the rural South. Roberts and Humbard were itinerant big-tent evangelists. They settled down—Roberts in Tulsa and Humbard in Akron.

In every case, their beginnings were solid. Their early sermons reflected it. Many of the cheerless people who listened, poor in spirit and poor in cash, identified with the televangelists' humble origins. And the listeners found balm and hope in the power of their sermons.

But to tune in on Swaggart, Bakker, and their brethren in recent years was to hear something less than an old-fashioned gospel sermon about sin, forgiveness, and revival. Instead, they pushed their colleges, their sons, their political agendas, their massive egos, and especially their survival.

The money poured in, and the televangelists' lifestyles and egos took quantum leaps. Robertson, Swaggart, Humbard, and Falwell founded colleges. Robertson, Roberts, Schuller, and Humbard all pushed their sons. Robertson technically resigned as head of CBN at the start of his 1988 presidential campaign, and son Tim succeeded him. Humbard used his young daughter to make blatantly embarrassing fund appeals. Roberts, Humbard, and Schuller tried to put the mantle of the ministry on their sons and posited them behind pulpits in front of the cameras. The sons clearly are not chips off the old blocks in their communication skills or charisma.

The televangelists often appealed for money by saying they would make the donors part of their ministry by bestowing phony titles. But the reality was that small groups, generally their immediate families, made all the decisions, and the televangelists were accountable to no one. My mother donated to a couple of these evangelists. After she died, we wrote and asked for a record of her donations. Of course, the letters went unanswered.

Along the way something had happened to the televangelists. As their illusions of being invincible and indispensable grew, and they became more and more insulated, their messages suffered. Folks heard precious little "gospel." The messages came to bear little resemblance to that of the biblical prophets and disciples, whose mantles these modern preachers claimed to wear.

Many listeners probably sensed it subconsciously. And when the donations started slipping, many of the televangelists simply hyped their shows and intensified their fund raising. They condemned everyone else for their problems, when they should have realized that, as Pogo used to say, "The enemy is us." They never reckoned with the possibility that the drop in donations was God's telling them it was time to get off the air.

The fallen televangelists seduced others. They engaged in phony fund appeals, always crying "Crisis!" even while maintaining lavish lifestyles and flouting the gospel's concern for the poor and oppressed. Always their words were draped in biblically laced language. Given their waning prayer lives they tried to wing it on their own sizable charisma, which was, circularly, a root of their problems.

Perhaps it was the men's departure from their basic messages and pushing their own personal agendas instead of the gospel that should have alerted more people that all was not well. But these televangelists' very successes insulated them from their vulnerabilities and from anyone who would talk straight to them. "If I have a problem, I'm not going to tell you about it," I once heard a televangelist say on his TV show. "I'm just going to take it to God." The staff of another televangelist were directed to weed out all critical letters sent to him. Few televangelists have had outside groups to blow the whistle on them. Because their boards were made up of family members and staff members beholden to them, when the temptations of money, sex, and power came, the televangelists had no one to help them battle those tantalizing lures.

Bakker went to prison. Humbard is off the air. Falwell has renounced politics. It is pitiful in retrospect to envision Swaggart driving up and down a row of seedy motels on a lonely search for gratification. Ironically, the lessons of these tragic events may have been the greatest sermons these men ever preached.

Lest we feel self-righteous by comparison, even the most committed among us face equally serious temptations, albeit of a different nature, perhaps. What are the Watergates each of us faces? Who among us can claim that we would have handled the temptations facing the televangelists any differently? There is more than enough vulnerability to go around.

Careerism

The hard-working person committed to doing a good job is especially vulnerable to the temptations that accompany power. That fits far too many of us, especially Americans, for we are hard workers. During my assignment overseas, I discovered something that surprised me. I learned that Americans work harder and longer and take fewer vacations than people in most industrial nations. The pace of living is much faster in America, and frequently, the quality of our workmanship is better. We're workaholics. This becomes a particularly subtle temptation to the abuse of power. Our job is often the vocational expression of our God-given talents and abilities. Our work is the locus of our power. And aren't hard work and good workmanship virtues?

We can become so consumed with our jobs or our ambition that we often succumb to a variety of temptations. I once wrote a short collection of biographies titled *Faith at the Top* (Elgin: David C. Cook, 1973). The jacket blurb read: "Meet ten men and women who dared to bring Christ along with them on their way to the top." Later both the title and the ad writer's blurb came to offend me. It was as if I were claiming: "If you have faith, you will get to the top," or, equally offensive, "If you are at the top, you must have had faith." The right use of power has little to do with gaining status or influence.

Too many people, even committed Christians, are so bent toward reaching a high position that they are willing to trample on others enroute to the top. Some years ago I was offered a White House assignment because the bureau chief wanted to reassign the reporter who was there at the time. I felt the reporter had done good work and didn't deserve to be taken off the beat. I didn't want any part of jerking him around—and I turned down the assignment. I thought, "Well, there goes my chance to cover the White House." Actually, I got a chance to cover the White House later, but even if I hadn't I felt I did the right thing by not responding to a chance to make a career leap at someone else's expense.

Ambition often devours the worker who is committed to a job and is eager to advance. Even more important, we can become so consumed with our jobs that we ignore our personal and family responsibilities. The boss,

the department chairman, the editor, the manager, who-
ever asks underlings to work longer hours or weekends
or holidays to accomplish tasks must consider the
expense to those employees and their families. How can
a boss be both loyal to the firm and sensitive to the subordinate's personal health and family responsibilities?

I was distressed to learn that the wife of one prominent evangelical Christian told their son, "I know Daddy's
gone a lot, but just remember he's doing it for the kingdom of God." What was the son to feel about his father?
About God? About himself and his own worth? Zeal for
one's calling must be tempered with equal passion for
one's personal and family relationships.

In my own life, I was single while I was covering
Watergate, an all-consuming assignment for more than
two years. I know that it would have been almost impossible to sustain both my Watergate assignment and a family. I count it as one of God's blessings that I had my two
beloved children at a time when my professional responsibilities were far less demanding, and I was able to spend
countless hours with them, morning and night, often middle of the night—many times my young daughter and I
had our best conversations then!—weekends, often aim-
lessly and with no agenda. I cherish those hours.

We parents hold nearly absolute power over our children. Yet many of us would be shocked to be told that we
are engaged in child abuse. We may not physically abuse
our children, but we emotionally abuse them through
neglect or by spending too little time with them or by
turning them over to baby-sitters or day care centers. We
try to rationalize this lack by saying our important
careers keep us from spending as much time with the
children as we would like. So we try to make the time we
do spend with them "quality" time, which means that we
feel pressured to cram a lot into those few hours, a pres-

sure transmitted to the children as well. Then parents and children alike feel anxiety. What really is called for is "quantity" time, lots and lots of unpressured, unhurried and unstructured time with the children. The curse of single-parent homes is a blight on the Christian community as well as elsewhere. But we must also face the hard fact that many of our Christian homes are de facto single-parent families because of the persistent absence of one parent or the other through careerism.

Avoiding the Abuse of Personal Power

How do we avoid abusing the power born of our talents and skills?

We must see that more important than reputation is character, as Mel Lorentzen of Wheaton College has frequently said. Our reputation is what others think of us; our character is what God sees. We must see ourselves clearly. We must know what truly is important and what is not; we must have our priorities in order.

There is a fundamental flaw in the notion that to be successful one must present the image of perfection. When the apostle Paul prayed for deliverance from his "thorn in the flesh," he said God told him: "My power is made perfect in weakness" (2 Cor. 12:9).

Swaggart was said to be addicted to pornography. It was not necessary to confess this on television. But had he dealt with it by seeking help through others, it probably would have enhanced his ministry, not mortally wounded it, and best, he might have conquered the addiction.

How do we avoid the temptations that result in self-deception and delusion and ultimately in assault, force, violence? Answers came to me as I was nearing the end of the semester in Harvard Business School's famed course "Power and Influence," which I had attended while a Fellow in Harvard's Institute of Politics. Using Harvard's vaunted case study approach, we had studied various forms of power and leadership and concluded with a look at power gone wrong. Instructors Todd Jick and Dan Isenberg spent the last session offering these tips on how the powerful can avoid the big fall:

Have a personal code of ethics.

Know yourself, your weaknesses, your strengths.

Avoid the illusion of invincibility. Several fallen corporate giants, they said, "began to believe they could do anything. They lost touch with reality." Have a "reality check."

"Have people on the outside who are not blinded by the same fantasy tell you when you're about to make a mistake." Have an accountability system.

Toward the end of class, one of the students made a comment. "If you're going to know what to do when you face a big ethical dilemma, you will have needed previously to make a lot of little ethical decisions," the student said. "You can't do long division and multiplication until you've learned how to add and subtract. We need daily practice being ethical to be able to deal with the big problems when they arise." In other words, if we have cut corners on the little matters along the way, when the big decisions come we will not be able to make the right choices.

Jick and Isenberg and the student were talking to future MBAs. But they might well have been talking to Jimmy Swaggart, Jim Bakker, and in fact, to all of us.

And we need models. Mine was my father. The apostle Paul wrote of Jesus as the perfect model: "who, though he was in the form of God, did not count equality with God a thing to be grasped, but emptied himself, taking

the form of a servant . . . humbled himself and became
obedient unto death" (Phil. 2:6–8).

Group Power

Christian organizations fall victim to the same kinds of
temptations as those facing individuals. They rail against
the sins that are sexual in nature, but not against the lust
of careerism and climbing the corporate ladder. These
days even religious organizations have "CEOs" and
"COOs," a revealing use of the world's nomenclature.
Many such Christian organizations are less proficient
than secular organizations in how they handle layoffs, the
hiring of minorities and women, and medical benefits.

Michael Timmis is a leader in Republican politics in
Michigan and a lawyer-businessman with interests in
fourteen states and a payroll of more than five thousand.
He also is a committed Christian.

"I can categorically state that I do not see any major
distinction between the operation of businesses and the
operation of Christian movements that would clearly dif-
ferentiate that one is Christ centered and the other is secular," Timmis says. "As a matter of fact, I think that the
businesses are often operated with more integrity than
some of the Christian movements I come in contact
with."[4]

Christian organizations often are very resistant to any
kind of criticism, and shield themselves from it by assert-
ing that any criticism is harmful to the kingdom of God.
They frequently take advantage of their employees by
arguing that they actually are working for the kingdom,
and thus they are paid less with fewer benefits. Christian
organizations may be self-perpetuating in their boards of

4. Speech to Conference for Young Evangelists 30–45, Leadership '88,
Washington, D.C., June 1988.

directors. Or, they have interlocking directorships. Several years ago, one man was the president of one Christian organization and a director of a second, while a colleague was president of the second organization and a director of the first.

Political Power

Power Can Degenerate into Force

Power is played out at the political level exactly the same way as at the personal or individual level, except on a grander scale.

At the national or international level, the sinful abuse of power can escalate into brute force, violence, and war. Power becomes a god. When Habakkuk protested the violence of the Chaldeans, the Lord told him their "power is their god" (1:11).

Modern Israel did not leap suddenly from being a democracy committed to the principles of the Law and the Prophets to being a police state. I was UPI's chief correspondent in Israel and senior Middle East correspondent from 1983 to 1986. I saw the national tragedy that gradually befell Israel, seemingly by inches. And that reminded me of how gradually we personally also slip into the wrongful use of power.

Israel was reborn in 1948 in the ashes of the Holocaust. Its founding fathers saw the new Israel, in the prophet's phrase, to be "a light to the nations" (Isa. 49:6), in that it would demonstrate to the world the biblical principles of justice, righteousness, and mercy. Indeed, in many ways it was. It was the only democracy in the Middle East, and early Israelis literally made a barren land to flower and streams to flow in the desert.

Yet the specter of the Holocaust never forsook them. Israel determined that never again would the Jewish people experience genocide. Nothing became more important to Israel than survival—not democratic principles, not the words of the Law or the Prophets. Instead, Israel developed what was considered to be the third strongest army on earth, behind only the United States and the Soviet Union.

The early years of reborn Israel were romantic, as captured in Leon Uris's *Exodus*. But every decade saw a war against the Arabs; few noticed that in almost every case the Israel Defence Forces (IDF) struck first. Then came the 1967 Six-Day War. This, too, was labeled Arab aggression, but when it was over Israel had captured the Golan Heights from Syria, the West Bank and East Jerusalem from Jordan, and the Sinai Peninsula and the Gaza Strip from Egypt.

Rightly or wrongly, the world began to look on Israel as a grabber of land. In 1981 the Israelis bombed a nuclear reactor under construction in Iraq. In 1982 the Israelis invaded southern Lebanon and occupied it militarily for three years. Had Israel become Goliath instead of David? What was happening to the Israeli psyche?

The Jaffe Center for Strategic Studies at Tel Aviv University asked 1,172 Israelis to identify the "guardian" in the text, "The guardian of Israel slumbers not, nor sleeps" (Ps. 121:4, Jaffe translation). According to the poll, 17 percent said it was God, 13 percent the State of Israel, 10 percent the United States, and 57 percent said the "guardian" was the Israeli army.

After my return from the Middle East, I wrote a book surveying the region. I felt it was a fair treatment of both the Israelis and the Arabs.[5] I pointed out that, contrary to popular assumption, more Arabs had died as a result

5. Wesley G. Pippert, *Land of Promise, Land of Strife: Israel at 40* (Waco: Word, 1988).

of Israeli violence than vice versa. The reaction was remarkable. Reviewers whose predominant loyalty lay with Israel—and if anything, I felt my book tilted slightly toward the Israelis—condemned me and accused me of misstating the facts of who had suffered more casualties at the hands of the other.

The same erosion that takes place in our personal moral character when we misuse power happened to the Israelis. They began to engage in massive retaliation in which the punishment was greater than the crime and to chip away at due process and collective (penalizing the group for the sins of the few) punishment. Their attitudes grew hard.[6]

My facts were accurate. In a typical incident, a Palestinian would throw a molotov cocktail at an Israeli bus, perhaps killing or wounding three or four persons. In retaliation, the Israelis would bomb a Palestinian guerrilla nest, often killing twenty or thirty. On Yom Kippur 1985, three Israelis were killed in a terrorist attack on their yacht moored off Cyprus. A few days later, Israeli war planes bombed the headquarters of the Palestine Liberation Organization in Tunisia, killing seventy-three. The Bible's admonition to take an arm for an arm (Exod. 21:24; Matt. 5:38–42) probably was intended to set a maximum limit to punishment or retaliation. In other words, if someone pokes you in the eye, you may not take more than an eye. But Israel breached this in the extreme. For an arm a life was taken; for three lives seventy-three were killed.[7]

The combination of this might and the zeal to survive proved to be lethal. The Palestinians' desire for a home-land—a desire as legitimate as the Jews'—erupted into the *intifadeh* in December 1987. With the world looking

6. Ibid., chapter 3, "The Problem Within," pp. 77–95.
7. Ibid.

on in horror, the Israeli might turned to force and violence, and Palestinians were killed by the hundreds. What had happened to the dream of modern Israel's founding fathers to be a light to the nations?

It is worth repeating: The worst outcome of waging war is not what we do to others but what we do to ourselves.

We are not innocent in America. We are an acknowledged violence-prone society where we teach children to play cops-and-robbers and cowboys-and-Indians, where riots are a part of the process of social change, where physical assault is the law of the street. There are few places in the world where there is as much violence as on certain American streets.

There surely is in our national psyche a worship of the military. Two presidents—George Washington and Dwight D. Eisenhower—understood this peril, and because they were generals their words carry extra weight in this regard. In his farewell address, Washington warned against "those overgrown military establishments, which under any form of government are inauspicious to liberty, and which are to be regarded as particularly hostile to republican liberty."

Nearly two centuries later Eisenhower, in his farewell address, said:

> We annually spend on military security more than the net income of all United States corporations. This conjunction of an immense military establishment and a large arms industry is new in the American experience. The total influence—economic, political, even spiritual—is felt in every city, every statehouse, every office of the federal government. We recognize the imperative need for this development. Yet we must not fail to comprehend its grave implications. Our toils, resources, and livelihood are all involved; so is the very structure of our society. In the councils of government, we must guard against the

acquisition of unwarranted influence, whether sought or unsought, by the military-industrial complex. The potential for the disastrous rise of misplaced power exists and will persist. We must never let the weight of this combination endanger our liberties or democratic processes.

Just War

The principles of a just war originated with the classical Greek and Roman philosophers like Plato and Cicero, and were expounded by Christian theologians like Ambrose, Augustine, and Thomas Aquinas. These principles include, among other conditions, that war must support a just cause, it must be declared by legitimate authority, it must be a last resort.

The principles of a just war make it extremely hard to justify almost any armed conflict. But President George Bush believed that the 1991 Persian Gulf war fit these criteria. "It has everything to do with what religion embodies: good versus evil, right versus wrong, human dignity and freedom versus tyranny and oppression. The war in the Gulf is not a Christian war, a Jewish war, or a Moslem war; it is a just war."[8] The fact that Saddam Hussein was such a vile man made it all the easier to label it a just war.

But was it a just war? A look at recent history demonstrates how much the Western world has subjugated the Middle East. For much of the eighteenth and nineteenth centuries, the British, French, Russians, and Germans trespassed the Middle East for their own selfish reasons. The British wanted to safeguard their shipping routes to India. The French were their great rival in the Middle East. Russia wanted a warm-water port, particularly Constantinople. The Germans, late starters, built rail-

---

8. George Bush, Speech to National Religious Broadcasters, January 28, 1991, *Weekly Compilation of Presidential Documents*, Vol. 27, No. 5, p. 87.

roads that economically threatened Britain and then struck up a relationship with the Ottoman Empire.

The cruel fact was that none of these Western powers cared very much for the Arab people—or even understood them.[9] The British did not understand either the fusion of religion and politics in Islam on the one hand, or the disunity and fragmentation of the Islamic world on the other.[10] The French did recognize this fusion, and used it to pit sect against sect, militia against militia, and one of the abhorrent results has been the decades-long civil war still going on in the old French mandate of Lebanon.

Particularly ignominious was the 1915 exchange of letters between the British high commissioner in Cairo, Sir Henry McMahon, and the sharif of Arabia, Hussein, in which the British promised the Arabs their independence after World War I if the Arabs would break with the Ottoman Empire and join the Allies. The Arabs did break with their brother Moslems and joined the Allies in the high hope this would lead to their independence. But almost at the very time of the exchange of letters, the British and French negotiated the secret Sykes-Picot agreement in which they decided on how the two Western powers would carve up the Middle East. This is what actually happened, and the League of Nations mandate made it official.[11]

Iraq and Jordan, for instance, were "lines drawn on an

---

9. See David Fromkin, *A Peace to End All Peace: The Fall of the Ottoman Empire and the Creation of the Modern Middle East* (New York: Henry Holt, 1989). The book was runner-up for the 1990 National Book Critics award.

10. Ibid., pp. 96–97, 104.

11. See George Antonius, *The Arab Awakening,* written in 1938 and reprinted in 1969 (Beirut: *Librairie du Liban*) and Albert Hourani, *The Emergence of the Modern Middle East* (Berkeley and Los Angeles: University of California Press, 1981), and his chapter, "The Arab Awakening Forty Years After."

empty map by British politicians" after World War I.[12] Britain even went so far as to install Hussein's son Feisal as king over Iraq. A British civil servant imposed the boundaries between Saudi Arabia, Kuwait, and Iraq.[13] Iraq gained its independence in 1932 but the British continued to meddle in its affairs for decades. Kuwait did not gain its independence until 1961.

One of the results of all this was a certain artificiality that the Western powers imposed on the Middle East. To paraphrase Gerald Nadler, one of my colleagues in the Middle East and a gifted writer with the ability to state something simply without sacrificing any of the complexity: "Most countries were a people before they became a nation; countries in the Middle East became nations before they were peoples."

The United States took a passive role during and after the key World War I period. But it aggressively took up the mantle of the British and French in 1990. One can almost understand why Saddam Hussein refers to the United States as the Great Satan. Hussein clearly was evil, but, given the history, his nature did not justify the United States' jingoistic display after its crushing defeat of him in the 100-hour land war. Clearly the United States' power had exploded into force.

The fact that the United States had so few casualties in the Persian Gulf war hardly justifies the war. Iraq lost a staggering number, estimated anywhere between 100,000 and 200,000 people—men, women, and children whom God also loves. The Kurds suffered. A just war?

In the case study of the Carter administration in chapter 3, we will look at that former president's analysis of *how* and *why* power degenerates into violence.

12. Fromkin, *A Peace to End All Peace*, 17.
13. Ibid., 17, 560.

The Loss of Power

Whether in the manipulation that comprises the abuse of personal power or in the force and violence that comprise the abuse of national power, the great tragedy is the loss of power itself.

Samson was one of the ancient Hebrew judges on whom the Spirit of the Lord had come (Judg. 14:19) so that he might deliver the Israelites from an adversary. He lost his power—symbolized by his physical strength—in his dalliance with the Philistine beauty, Delilah.

I have in my life witnessed the deaths of four persons. One was my mother, one of the godliest persons I have ever known, who passed away in the arms of her youngest son, Harold, with four generations in the room. I saw two die in the Cook County electric chair in Chicago. The fourth was in Israel. One Sunday afternoon, as I was standing on our balcony in the Jerusalem neighborhood of Abu Tor, I noticed a disturbance on the main Jerusalem-Hebron highway that passed a block away. An old and dusty Arab bus, easily identifiable by its green-gray markings, had stalled on the incline of a small hill, and a crowd was gathering. Sensing something, I ran to the scene. A Palestinian young man lay in a pool of blood in the middle of the street, his whitened skin indicating profound shock. He was obviously near death. The bus had a gaping hole. It later came to light that a young Israeli soldier, seeking revenge for the slaying of two Israeli collegians in Arab woods near Bethlehem a few days earlier, had hidden on the hillside and fired a rocket-propelled grenade into the bus. Ten Arabs were wounded, the young man mortally.

Ponder the sum cost of the violence: two Israeli collegians and an Arab young man who was revealed to have been an honors graduate student in engineering dead, and nine suffering from injuries.

In a great Christmas sermon preached at the start of World War II, Harry Emerson Fosdick spoke eloquently of the cost of force and violence. He told a story that occurred in 1805 when Napoleon bombarded Vienna. "The shells struck the Jesuit grammar school. One of the students, an eight-year-old boy, was in his room practicing on the piano, and in terror he fell to the floor and hid his face. Then in a moment came the voice of one of the schoolmasters, calling through the corridor, 'Schubert, Franz Schubert, are you all right?'"

Nine years later, Fosdick related, the Russian and Austrian armies invaded Italy. In one village the women fled to the church for safety, but the soldiers followed them even there, and slew them before the altar. "One mother, however, with an infant at her breast, hid in the belfry and saved her child. That infant was Verdi, the composer. And now most of us could not tell a single thing about those decisive battles—not one—but we are listening still to *Rigoletto, Aïda, La Traviata, Il Trovatore.*"

Fosdick pointed out that Herod nearly killed the infant Jesus. "That is what war does all the time, and poverty, and slums, and all our social cruelties. They kill decisive babies."[14]

Who can calculate the talents and skills of the fallen in war and what might have been accomplished through them? This is also the tragedy of abortion. No one will ever know what the aborted babies might have achieved in our world. Consider the babies who are born but live underprivileged and oppressed lives and never get a chance to discover their abilities and develop them. How many Mstislav Rostropoviches are there in the world

14. Harry Emerson Fosdick, "The Decisive Babies of the World," *Living Under Tension: Sermons on Christianity Today* (New York: Harper & Brothers, 1941), pp. 224, 229.

who perhaps could play the cello as well as he but simply have never had the chance to take even one music lesson? Might not another have found a cure for cancer? For AIDS? How many Schuberts and Verdis and Jonas Salks have died before their talents were allowed to flower? These, too, are victims of others' power abuses.

The finest swimmer and one of the best natural athletes I have ever known was a boy in my hometown. Oscar was poor, and it was clear he would have neither the encouragement nor the means to go on to higher education. Instead, it was I who got the chance to go on to college and learn to swim under a future Olympics coach, Dr. Jim Counsilman. And how important was that to me? After years of trying I am only an average swimmer at best.

The abuse of power leads to the loss of power, one's own or of innocent others. And that is a tragedy of incalculable proportions.

Case Study
Watergate

On a hot Saturday, June 17, 1972, I was on the desk in UPI's Washington bureau. A short story came in. Five men wearing rubber gloves had been arrested while breaking into the Democratic national offices in the Watergate complex in Washington. I routinely edited and filed it on the wire as did almost all of the media that day.

Twenty-six months later, when the story ended with President Richard Nixon's resignation, America had suffered its most serious internal crisis since the Civil War. It stalled the apparatus of the federal government at a time when there were other domestic crises over inflation and energy. Worse, it caused the people of America to have deep suspicions about the basic institutions of their government, and made mockery of the Constitution and the Bill of Rights. It cast a pall over Nixon's noble attempts to bring "a generation of peace" through opening the doors to Mainland China and the Soviet Union, the communist goliaths of the period. It made a mockery of "law and order."

What had happened?

Background: The Turbulence of the 1960s

Tumult and upheaval spread throughout the United States in the 1960s. It proved to be the greatest revolution in America since the Civil War exactly a century earlier. The signs were kaleidoscopic. There was a sad toll of

75

assassinations: John F. Kennedy, Martin Luther King, Jr., Robert F. Kennedy, Malcolm X, George Lincoln Rockwell. Riots charred Watts, Newark, Detroit, and other American inner cities; the bitter, winless Vietnam war was fought in a far-away land. A massive disillusionment with the fabled American dream infected every institution, ranging from the federal government to big corporations to the organized church.

This was the decade when war babies and older baby boomers dropped out of church. Church attendance traditionally had been above 40 percent. But in the 1960s, while their parents and older siblings continued to attend church in only slightly smaller figures, the young people born in the 1940s and 1950s stayed away; only one in three war babies and older baby boomers attended worship.[1]

There were a few redeeming features. The civil rights movement led to passage of the first body of civil rights legislation since the Civil War. After the halcyon years of the 1950s Americans had been forced to be introspective about the direction their land was taking. After the turbulence of the 1960s the country was ready for peace and quiet, for "law and order" in the best sense of that battered phrase.

But the Watergate scandal lay ahead.

Richard Nixon and His Men

Richard Nixon had been reborn as a political candidate after losing the election for president in 1960 and governor of California in 1962.

"Bring us together," candidate Nixon had proclaimed in the 1968 campaign. Nixon himself seemed to tell Americans that a reverence for God and the biblical val-

1. Wesley G. Pippert, "The Revival of Religion in America," *Editorial Research Reports*, July 22, 1988.

ues of justice and mercy would be at the heart of his administration. He established Sunday worship services in the White House. His family was virtuous to the point of being almost Victorian. Nixon seemed disciplined and austere in his private life, in sharp contrast to his two lusty, earthy predecessors.

After the turbulence of the decade, it seemed the nation was eager to take to heart his 1969 inaugural plea to "lower our voices." Some even dared to hope the government would follow his promise in the same speech "to listen in new ways to the voices of quiet anguish, the voices that speak without words, the voices of the heart, to the injured voices, the anxious voices, the voices that have despaired of being heard."

But once Nixon was in office, the atmosphere of his administration was shockingly different.

Nixon and his men were bent on much tougher measures to quell the disquiet of the sixties. In 1970 Nixon approved the Huston plan—named for Tom Huston, the young aide who drafted it—for domestic intelligence-gathering that included breaking and entering, mail interception, and other covert activities. The White House assembled an "enemies" list. The president secretly taped all his official conversations and telephone calls.

The list of "White House horrors," as John N. Mitchell, then the attorney general, repeatedly called them later, seemed endless. The atmosphere had been befouled. The June 1972 Watergate break-in was, tragically, the logical next development.

The first event that led directly to the Watergate break-in was the establishment of the "White House plumbers" to investigate security leaks. To prevent the public from learning more about the United States' involvement in the Vietnam war, the "plumbers" rifled the office of Pentagon Papers defendant Daniel Ellsberg's psychiatrist.

Ellsberg had leaked the Pentagon Papers, a secret document on the origins of the Vietnam war, to the *New York Times*. The "plumbers" wanted to get Ellsberg's notes to his therapist, leak derogatory information about Ellsberg, and destroy his credibility. The operation was financed by a political contribution that Charles Colson, Nixon's liaison to special interest groups, had obtained from the dairy industry.

The second event that led directly to the Watergate break-in came in early 1972. John N. Mitchell, the nation's top law-enforcement official and the symbol of "law and order," discussed with the general counsel of the Finance Committee to Reelect the President (FCRP), G. Gordon Liddy, his $250,000 "Gemstone" plan for gathering "political intelligence" about the Democrats in the 1972 campaign. Mitchell approved.

The Watergate operation was under way, directed by Liddy and financed by funds from the FCRP.

The Cover-Up

Within hours after the burglary team members were arrested, the top White House and reelection committee staff members scrambled to shield themselves. Within days President Nixon talked with his chief of staff, H. R. Haldeman, about interfering with the investigation of the break-in by contending national security was involved. Following up, Haldeman suggested to the FBI that its investigation might uncover CIA operations, proposing unsubtly that the FBI call off its dogs. The CIA replied that it had nothing to do with Watergate. Twenty-six months later, when the Supreme Court ordered the release of the White House tapes, Nixon's conversation with Haldeman became the "smoking gun" that forced Nixon to resign on August 9, 1974.

Meanwhile, during the summer and fall of 1972, Democrat George McGovern had campaigned futilely, his charges about high-level involvement in Watergate falling on deaf ears. Nixon was overwhelmingly elected and inaugurated in January 1973.

An ironic footnote: On the Sunday following the inauguration, with Nixon, Mitchell, Haldeman, Colson, domestic affairs adviser John Ehrlichman, and others in attendance, Billy Graham preached in the White House East Room. I was there as a reporter. Graham preached against the sins of pornography and obscenity and offered a proposal to recite the Ten Commandments in school classrooms as an alternative to the controversial mandatory prayers.

Earlier in January 1973 the five obscure men who made up the burglary team had been convicted in a short trial as being the sole perpetrators. To assure their silence following the burglary, with the approval of Mitchell and Haldeman, they had been promised bail, legal expenses, and family support, to be paid out of $350,000 in campaign funds that had been secreted at the White House. But after the January trial their demands for more money kept coming. The tension among the Nixon men was becoming untenable.

March 1973 came. It was the beginning of the end. The Watergate cover-up began to unravel as the original defendants stepped up their demands for more money and clemency. White House Counsel John Wesley Dean III warned Nixon that "a cancer is growing on the presidency." Two days later James McCord, the security director for the reelection committee and the wiretapper on the burglary team, wrote Chief United States District Court Judge John J. Sirica that perjury had been committed during the January trial. Dean, unwilling to accept hints that he take the rap, resigned and started talking to

United States Attorney Earl Silbert, the chief prosecutor at the time. The rumor mill shifted into high gear.

It was at this time that I was assigned full time to the Watergate story, about the same time that other media also assigned reporters to the story. I was principal UPI reporter on Watergate, and it consumed most of my waking hours from March 1973 until New Year's Day 1975, when the jury returned guilty verdicts in the trial of the major figures.

Nixon's men began to fall. On April 30, 1973, I was sitting in Colson's office when word came that Nixon's top two aides, H. R. Haldeman and John Ehrlichman, had resigned, as had Attorney General Richard G. Kleindienst, and John Dean had been fired. Shock waves went throughout the government.

In May the Senate Watergate committee began public hearings. Archibald Cox was appointed by Attorney General Elliott Richardson as special prosecutor to take over the investigation. In one particularly dark episode, Richardson and Deputy Attorney General William Ruckelshaus resigned before Solicitor General Robert Bork finally carried out Nixon's orders to fire Cox. The mass exodus came to be known as the "Saturday night massacre." I have been in Washington a quarter of a century and I never before nor since have observed the sense of panic that I did that October night.

It ended in hundreds of courtroom proceedings, with the new special prosecutor, Leon Jaworski, pressing on toward the truth. Vice President Agnew; four Cabinet members—Mitchell, who had been director of Nixon's finance reelection committee, Commerce Secretary Maurice Stans, Kleindienst, and Treasury Secretary John B. Connally; a host of White House and reelection committee aides; and a host of corporation and cooperative executives all faced the law of the land.

Twenty-six months after the break-in, the House Judiciary Committee wrote the death notice of the Nixon years in its three articles of impeachment:

Obstruction of justice in the Watergate cover-up. This article led to the uncovering of all of the other persons involved.

A general misuse of power. This was far more serious, for it cited actions that undermined the constitutional rights of every American citizen and undermined the nation's law enforcement and intelligence agencies.

Defiance of the power of impeachment given to Congress by the Constitution.

A few days later Nixon resigned. In the end Nixon told the nation merely: "Throughout the long and difficult period of Watergate, I have felt it was my duty to persevere. . . . In the past few days, however, it has become evident to me that I no longer have a strong enough political base in Congress to justify continuing that effort. . . . Sometimes I have succeeded and sometimes I have failed."[2]

Nixon showed courage but no confession, regret but no remorse.

Finally, on a gray day in August 1974, Marine Helicopter One lifted Richard M. Nixon and his family off the South lawn of the White House over the heads of hundreds of persons and swung around the Washington Monument on its way to Andrews Air Force Base, where Air Force One would take them home to California to stay.

A month later President Ford pardoned Nixon. By coincidence, I was having breakfast that day with George

2. Address to the American People, August 7, 1974, *Weekly Compilation of Presidential Documents*, Vol. 10, No. 32, August 12, 1974, p. 1015.

McGovern, whose presidential campaign had been the immediate reason for the Watergate excesses. A few Sundays later, my pastor, Dr. Edward W. Bauman, said from the pulpit that President Ford had done Richard Nixon no favor, because by pardoning him before there was contrition Ford interrupted that painful process of suffering that might have brought Nixon to acknowledge his wrongdoing and then to repentance.

Why Watergate?

What had happened? Why did it happen? Where were the pride and conscience in serving one's government?

A cesspool of despicable patterns of behavior had pervaded the Nixon administration: a fear and suspicion that all of the nation's ills could be traced to the cold-war foe, communism; a paranoia that led the White House to view political opponents as enemies; a fundamental distrust that, despite the outward professions of team play and loyalty, led the top members of the administration to secretly wiretap each other, pass the buck whenever something went wrong, and turn on each other with almost cannibalistic vengeance, brother turning on brother—as in President Nixon's sanctioned wiretapping of Donald Nixon; an undermining of the hallowed Bill of Rights. The scandal revealed the distrust, zeal, and excessive pragmatism that had festered in the White House and the Committee to Reelect the President. The Watergate cover-up had occurred in the Oval Office itself, the ignoble and tragic end to what had begun slightly more than four years earlier as a bright hope in the hearts and minds of Americans.

At the pinnacle of its power and popularity the Nixon Administration observed fearfully the distrust and demonstrations of the sixties in the land. But their reaction was worse than what they had feared. They had become so infected with the lust of power that they suppressed any response of sensitivity and compassion they might have had, and instead followed their Machiavellian way of thinking that the end justified the means. They had created such an atmosphere that wiretaps and Watergates, break-ins and dirty tricks were inevitable.

Where were the lawyers, professionals who were supposed to know the difference between what was lawful and what was not? President Nixon; Vice President Spiro T. Agnew; Attorney General John N. Mitchell; White House Counsel John W. Dean III; White House Special Counsel Charles W. Colson; Attorney General Richard G. Kleindienst; Gordon Liddy, former counsel of the Committee to Reelect the President and mastermind of the Watergate break-in; Donald Segretti, the reelection committee's "dirty trickster"; Gordon Strachan, Egil Krogh, and David Young, former White House staffers—all were lawyers and all were charged with Watergate crimes. It led Dean to remark during the hearings, "How in God's name could so many lawyers get involved in something like this?"[3]

Where was the press, which is supposed to be the public watchdog? Few reporters paid much attention to the story, with the notable exceptions of those from the *Washington Post,* the *Los Angeles Times,* and CBS. I experienced this indifference firsthand. Despite the absence of many solid news stories, rumors were rife around Washington. I was in charge of the UPI Washington bureau during the Republican National Convention in Miami Beach in late August 1972, and I assigned a reporter full time to the Watergate story. After the convention, when Labor Day came, I was assigned to the

---

3. *Hearings before the Select Committee on Presidential Campaign Activities, U.S. Senate, 93rd Congress* (Washington, D.C.: Government Printing Office, 1973), 3:1054.

McGovern presidential campaign, and when I arrived back in town after the initial two-week campaign swing, I found the reporter I assigned had been taken off Watergate. The press played a major role in uncovering the scandals in late 1972 and 1973, but what was it doing during those earlier years when the seeds that bore the bitter fruit of Watergate were sown?

Where was the clergy? Had liberal theologians, by proclaiming an age of situational ethics and moral relativism, unwittingly helped produce Watergate? Had evangelical theologians been seduced by Nixon's virtuous prose? What if Billy Graham had preached against the sin of lust for power—Christ's first temptation, we recall—on those Sundays in the White House East Room instead of the Ten Commandments?

Something had gone wrong, tragically wrong, in the Nixon White House in the short years of its life. But there was plenty of the guilt of indifference to go around.

Perhaps Nixon's new chief of staff, Alexander M. Haig, unwittingly came closest to explaining the cause. An eighteen-minute gap had been discovered in the White House tapes of Nixon's conversations, and Judge Sirica held hearings to find out whether the gap had occurred accidentally or whether an incriminating conversation had been intentionally erased. Testifying on December 6, 1973, Haig speculated that the gap may have been caused by "some sinister force." The first syllable of the middle word of Haig's phrase may have struck the truth of the matter.

The Moral Dimension: Arrogance of Power

When the media finally awakened to the story, we reported in excruciating detail about the break-in, the White House tapes, Richard Nixon's finances, and his private, foul language. Seldom if ever has a public official been as closely scrutinized by the media as he was. But we were much less skillful in defining why Watergate occurred, what it is that makes those who have power so vulnerable to abusing it and so greedy in wanting to expand it. These were moral questions to understanding Watergate, and we dealt with them inadequately if at all.

Sometimes I asked Watergate defendants in the sidewalk news conferences we held outside the United States District Courthouse in Washington whether they felt any remorse. Invariably they scorned the question, exhibiting the moral bankruptcy that characterized the Nixon administration.

The Nixon Men

A parade of men (always they were men and not women) were convicted or pleaded guilty in court in a long series of legal actions. Following are capsule glimpses of a few of them:

Jeb Stuart Magruder at age thirty-four was a young man in a hurry. He had been on his way toward becoming vice president of Jewel Tea Company, one of the nation's largest retailers, and he had started two small cosmetics companies. Then a call came from the White House. He went to President Nixon's palatial estate at San Clemente, California, for an interview. In vivid but alarming terms Magruder described how he felt afterward: "As I drove up the coast with the summer sun falling into the ocean off to my left, my hands were trembling. I was an ambitious man, a man with a craving for power, and I wanted, more than I had ever wanted anything, to return to work in that world of power and challenge."[4] Four years later Magruder was in jail.

---

4. Jeb Stuart Magruder, *An American Life: One Man's Road to Watergate* (New York: Atheneum, 1974), pp. 9–10.

As the cover-up began to unravel in March 1973, rumors quickly focused on Magruder, by then an assistant secretary of commerce after having served as deputy communications director at the White House and deputy director of the reelection committee. I got an interview with Magruder that month. He asked me to come surreptitiously in a side door of the Commerce Department, and he asked that he be identified in the story only as "a source close to the investigation," which, ironically, was absolutely accurate. After the interview was over, he asked me if I could shred my notes. Actually the story he gave me was misleading,[5] contending that the money he had handled was intended to cover security precautions taken against anticipated disruptions of the convention in Miami Beach. As it turned out, at the time Magruder talked to me he was close to capitulating. Within days he had hired a lawyer and was talking to the prosecutors.

Magruder's lust for power may have had other unfortunate spinoffs. In his book he writes that he had encounters with or did not get along with Colson,[6] White House Press Secretary Ron Ziegler,[7] Liddy,[8] Hugh Sloan,[9] and Dean,[10] to name only a few.

"Don't you think in this area that individuals should have personal ethics whose requirements exceeded the strict letter of the law?" Senator Sam Ervin asked Hugh Sloan, the straight-arrow treasurer of the Finance Committee to Reelect the President and former White House aide.

"Yes, sir," Sloan replied.[11] Sloan had resigned soon after the break-in and had begun to cooperate fully with

5. Thus, I no longer feel bound by the ground rules of the interview.
6. Magruder, *An American Life*, p. 64.
7. Ibid., pp. 61-62.
8. Ibid., pp. 170-178.
9. Ibid., pp. 142, 232.
10. Ibid., p. 248.
11. *Hearings*, 2:570.

the investigation. He testified that when he expressed concern over the large amounts of money he was being asked to turn over for unknown purposes, White House aide Dwight Chapin told him he was "overwrought."[12]

Sloan was not charged and emerged as one of the first heroes of the ordeal. After he resigned, he never submitted to interviews, he did not write a book, and he resumed his totally private life.

Bart Porter, age thirty-three, was typical of the bright, ambitious young men who worked in the White House. He was a former Marine officer and was confident to the point of cockiness. Magruder defined him in these put-down words: "He's been in the White House and gotten a taste of the limousines and all the other amenities and he wanted to have them on his own. He and I often discussed his ambitions, which if not well focused were nonetheless large."[13]

Porter had become the scheduling director for the committee to reelect the president. When he testified to the Senate Watergate committee he said, "I did not do it for money. I did not take a bribe. I did not do it for power. I did not do it for position.

"Yet," Porter went on, "my vanity was appealed to. . . . I think all of those things coupled with what I have found to be a weakness in my character, quite frankly, to succumb in that pressure, all added up to my tipping over to the other side."

He pointed out the personal cost of Watergate to him: "I have been terminated from a lucrative position."

Ervin replied to him, "It was a wise man named William Shakespeare who wrote a play called *Henry IV* (sic) and in that he has one of his characters, Cardinal

12. Ibid., 2:545.
13. Magruder, *An American Life*, p. 234.

Wolsey, say . . . 'Had I but served my God with half the
zeal I served my king, he would not in mine age have left
me naked to mine enemies.'"[14]

Former New York cop Anthony T. Ulascewicz testified
glibly that he investigated the sexual, drinking, domestic,
and social habits of Nixon's opponents and other political figures while he was on the White House staff.

"Would it be fair to say you dealt in dirt at the direction of the White House?" Senator Lowell P. Weicker, Jr.,
asked.

"Allegations of it, yes, sir," Ulascewicz testified.

"Political dirt?" Weicker asked.

"All right, sir," Ulascewicz said.[15]

Just before Christmas 1973 I interviewed Charles
Colson as he sat in blue pin-striped shirtsleeves at his
oval desk in an ultramodernistic office two blocks from
the White House. He was now representing the Team-
sters Union and was under investigation but had not yet
pleaded guilty. His conversion to Christ had only recently
become known. This exchange took place:

Q: What was the sin of Watergate?
Colson: (long pause) I don't think I want to answer that,
not for the record certainly. I could write a book about
that.
Q: Do you think the atmosphere—
Colson: Arrogance was the great sin of Watergate, the
great sin of a lot of us, probably my greatest. That was
the chapter in C. S. Lewis's book [*Mere Christianity*] that
had the greatest impact on me. I think the great sin all
of us are guilty of, and it's the hardest one to recognize,
is admiring our own egos, our own selves, really believ-
ing that we as individuals have capacities that we some-

14. *Hearings*, 2:676. Ervin was quoting *King Henry VIII*, act 3, scene 2.
15. Ibid., 6:2275-2276.

how develop in ourselves. We really are children of God in the sense that we can really do only what God gives us the capacity to do. It is his power, not ours, that determines our destiny.[16]

A few months later, Colson walked into the courtroom of U.S. District Court Judge Gerhard Gesell—I was there on assignment —and pleaded guilty to the obstruction of justice. He told the judge, "It was this attitude of 'not caring,' this callousness to the rights of a defendant that gave rise to the crime to which I am now pleading." Minutes afterward, Colson stood outside the courthouse and told us reporters, "I've committed my life to Christ. . . . I can work for the Lord in prison or out of prison."

Colson went on to great heights and maturity as a prison reformer and a spokesman for evangelical Christianity.

Senator Sam Ervin: Moral Perspective

The Senate Watergate hearings, chaired by a self-styled "country lawyer" Senator Sam J. Ervin, Jr., provided the moral definition of the Nixon administration's wrongful use of power.

It was just before noon at the Senate Watergate hearings in the ornate Senate caucus room. Frederick C. LaRue, a millionaire land developer from Jackson, Mississippi, and a former special consultant to President Nixon, as well as a former special assistant to campaign director John N. Mitchell, was finishing his testimony.

Chairman Ervin turned to him and said, "I can't resist the temptation to philosophize just a little bit about the Watergate. The evidence thus far introduced, presented

16. The interview in its entirety was carried on the prime UPI-AAA wire about December 24, 1973.

before this committee, tends to show that men upon whom fortune had smiled benevolently, and who possessed great financial power, undertook to nullify the laws of men and the laws of God for the purpose of gaining what history will call a very temporary political advantage. The evidence also indicates that possibly the efforts to nullify the laws of men might have succeeded if it had not been for a courageous federal judge, Judge Sirica, and a very untiring set of investigative reporters.

"But I come from a state like that of the state of Mississippi where they have great faith in the fact that the laws of God are imparted in the King James Version of the Bible. And I think that those who participated in this effort to nullify the laws of men and the laws of God overlooked one of the laws of God which is set forth in the seventh verse of the sixth chapter of Galatians: 'Be not deceived; God is not mocked; for whatsoever a man soweth, that shall he also reap.'"[17]

Ervin brushed aside former Commerce Secretary Maurice Stans' argument that previous administrations also had engaged in similar wrongdoing. "There have been murder and larceny in every generation, but that hasn't made murder meritorious or larceny legal," Ervin retorted.[18]

"I want to mention a little of the Bible, a little of history and a little of law. The concept embodied in the phrase, 'every man's home is his castle,' represents the realization of one of the most ancient and universal hungers of the human heart. One of the prophets described the mountain of the Lord as being a place where every man might dwell under his own vine and fig tree with none to make him afraid.[19]

17. *Hearings*, 6:2343–2344.
18. Ibid., 2:756.
19. Ibid., 6:2630–2631. Ervin was quoting Micah 4: 2, 4.

"One of the greatest statements ever made by any statesman—that was William Pitt the Elder, and before this country revolted against the King of England—he said this: 'The poorest man in his cottage may bid defiance to all the forces of the crown. It may be frail, its roof may shake, the wind may blow through it, the storm may enter, the rain may enter, but the King of England cannot enter. All his force dares not cross the threshold of the ruined tenements.'

"And yet we are told here today, and yesterday, that what the King of England cannot do, the President of the United States can."[20]

The sharpest, overall analysis of the abuse of power also came from, of course, Sam Ervin. "It is proof of what my old philosophy professor told me, that the greatest trials we have in this world is [sic] when you are compelled to choose between different loyalties," Ervin said.[21]

"I can suggest to future people . . . they may be rightly or wrongly judged by the standards set out in the Scriptures where it says, 'Men love darkness rather than light, because their deeds are evil,'" Ervin said.[22]

20. Ibid.
21. Ibid., 1: 283.
22. Ibid., 2:628. Ervin was quoting John 3:19.

3

Power as Servant

The Sunday after he won the 1976 Democratic presidential nomination in Madison Square Garden, Jimmy Carter went back to Plains, Georgia, and as he frequently did, taught Sunday school. He talked about the servant:

> A great, strong, sure person need not prove it always. That's the way it is with Christ. And that's the way it is with Christians. When you're sure of your strength, you can exhibit compassion, emotion, love, concern, equality—and, even better than equality, the attitude of a servant. You can say, I'm not only better than you, you're better than I am. And I want to work with you.[1]

The concept of servant is full of paradoxes:
Traditionally, we think of the servant as a slave, subjugated, powerless, oppressed. This is easy to grasp.

1. Men's Bible Class, Plains Baptist Church, July 18, 1976. See full text of Carter's lesson in Wesley G. Pippert, *The Spiritual Journey of Jimmy Carter* (New York: Macmillan, 1978), pp. 162–175.

On the other hand, we assert that the servant also has power, often great power, that can be wielded even over those with much more authority. We think here of the power of the peasant to prevail ultimately over the oppressor, or, the power that the one who serves our creature-needs has over us.

Finally, in our discussion, the ideal servant is the person vested with great authority who uses power to serve and care for others. For an individual, this might mean merely being a good neighbor; for the leader of a nation, this surely would mean the pursuit of justice and peace for the land.

In sorting out these notions, I merely make note of the servant as a slave. I will discuss the other two concepts in more detail—why the servant has power, and why the servant who cares for others, perhaps by simply being a good neighbor or by pursuing justice, models the right exercise of power.

The Servant as Powerful

The prophet Isaiah articulated the power of the people long before the political philosophers of our day: "He gives power to the faint, and to him who has no might he increases strength" (40:29).

"Fear not," the Lord says repeatedly. "Fear not, you worm Jacob, you men of Israel! . . . Behold, I will make of you a threshing sledge, new, sharp, and having teeth; you shall thresh the mountains and crush them, and you shall make the hills like chaff" (41:14–15).

Ultimately the servant is powerful.

In a limited way we can illustrate how the servant has power. The small obligations in life can really loom in importance: preparing our meals, seeing that our children are cared for while we attend to our public duties, sewing on missing buttons before we are seen by other people, being sure our cars will run when we turn on the ignition. These chores we can subordinate to underlings, often by hiring someone to handle them. Minor, very minor, you say. But what happens when we miss a meal or two? Or face the embarrassment of looking a little tacky? Or have a flight to catch and our car stalls? And as for children, what public duty can possibly be more important than they are? I submit that in those instances restaurant cooks, baby-sitters, housekeepers, mechanics have the real power in our lives, greater than our own.

Servants tend to help us in the areas of our creature comforts and in those tasks that we either disdain or for which we lack ability to perform. When we go to other people to look after our needs—physical, spiritual, or emotional—we give them authority over a part of our existence. Servants use their own special abilities to help us in our weaknesses and in so doing become more powerful than we are. In a real way we delegate to them their power over us.

Harriet Goldhor Lerner, a psychotherapist at the Menninger Clinic, points out that all of us—whether servant or master—share the power to act and to make choices, "And this, in the end, is the only real power we have."[2]

One section of the Bible that defies all logic is the "suffering-servant" passages of the Book of Isaiah (49; 52: 13–53). The paradox is this: The passages portray the Lord, the omniscient, omnipotent God, as a *servant*. How can a powerful God be a servant?

Greenleaf looks at servanthood from the standpoint of those being served: "The best test, and most difficult to administer, is: do those served grow as persons; do they,

---

2. Harriet Goldhar Lerner, *The Dance of Anger: A Woman's Guide to Changing the Patterns of Intimate Relationships* (New York: Harper & Row, 1985), p. 66.

while being served, become healthier, wiser, freer, more autonomous, more likely themselves to become servants?"[3] More often than not, I fear, we use servants not to help us grow but for just the opposite reasons: to help us put aside dealing with the weaknesses in our lives or to bolster our own sense of power over the servants.

On the other hand, when we cast ourselves in the servant role, such as by helping others with tasks or listening to their problems, we are in situations fraught with temptation. In doing these things, we run the risk of wrongfully assuming a certain superiority; we split our focus, assigning ourselves an importance in our roles that can overshadow our concern for the good of those we help. This can lead to pride. Once again, persons with certain skills and in certain vocations are especially vulnerable to this temptation—pastors, counselors, politicians, entertainers.

The Servant as an Agent of Justice

But temptations or no, all of us are called to serve. And the key way we serve in a broken world is by the ministration of justice.

Two memorials in the city I have called home for a quarter of a century capture the essence of power as servant or the pursuit of justice. The memorial built on Capitol Hill to Senator Robert A. Taft quotes his words: "Let us see that the state is the servant of the people, and that the people are not the servants of the state." Downtown, overlooking the Tidal Basin, the words of Thomas Jefferson are etched in his memorial: "Indeed I tremble for my country when I reflect that God is just, that his justice cannot sleep forever."

3. Robert K. Greenleaf, *The Servant as Leader* (Cambridge, Mass.: Center for Applied Studies, 1973), p. 7. The emphasis is Greenleaf's.

God thinks of justice in very realistic ways. In chapter 1 we discussed the Hebrew word מִשְׁפָּט that often occurs as "judgment" or mere justice in the English translations. The modern translation has legal implications: Justice is not an ethereal idea but something very pragmatic and practical that deals with legislation, bureaucratic regulations, court orders. It is a mistake to overspiritualize what the Bible means by justice. In the same Sunday school lesson after the Democratic convention, Jimmy Carter also spoke about justice. Quoting 1 John 4:16, "God is love," he said: "Love in isolation doesn't mean anything. But love, if applied to other people, can change their lives for the better through simple justice—fairness, equality, concern, compassion, redressing of grievances, elimination of inequalities, recognizing the poor are the ones who suffer the most even in our society which is supposed to be fair."

My family have demonstrated to me what it means to be just and merciful. My father, a farmer, was a good neighbor in the sense that only rural people fully grasp. He helped people who needed help. He signed a note to help a hard-pressed neighbor, a foolish act by worldly standards, even though he knew the neighbor might not repay (and he didn't). My eldest brother, Charles, would leave his own harvest to help a distressed neighbor. Chuck would spend the entire night at the bedside of a person who was dying, and leave at dawn to go work a full day without a break. My sister Marie has opened her home and spread her table to uncounted persons.

My two small children have taught me another lesson: The act of mercy must not be done in a grudging or a disciplinary way, but courteously and in a friendly fashion. We often ride Metro, the Washington subway, and at the top of the escalator at our stop, the same man always stands with a can in his hand for contributions. The children always want to drop in a coin. So I, too, drop in my coin and hurry on wordlessly. But David, age four, who has irrepressible glee, always stops to engage the man in happy banter. David's attention clearly cheers the man far more than his small contribution does. The other night we were at a filling station when a young man, his blonde hair blowing in the wind, asked me for a dollar for gas. I indicated clearly that I was skeptical as he described his plight—but eventually I gave him the dollar. Later, driving down the street, I talked to the children. "We always want to help the poor," I said, "but sometimes we don't know if they are really needy or want to spend it on something foolish." Then I pointed out that in the case of the young man at the filling station I had given him the dollar. "But Daddy," Elizabeth, age six, said, "You weren't polite to him." I haven't forgotten the insights those children had that I didn't. The act of mercy always ought to be done in a way that is loving and joyful as well.

Justice as Fairness, Righteousness, and Mercy

U.S. Representative Paul B. Henry, a political scientist, defines the inter-relationship of love, justice, and power in this way: "Politics, rooted in power, nevertheless fulfills a legitimate function when it serves the claims of justice. Love, while rejecting power and going beyond the rights and duties established by justice, establishes a will for justice and a moral motivation which crowns the just act. Love, while personally mediated, complements justice with its objective demands."[4]

The God-given purpose of power is to seek and do justice.

We sometimes tend to think of justice as referring only to punishment. "He got his just desserts," we say glibly.

4. Paul B. Henry, "Love, Power and Justice," *The Christian Century*, November 23, 1977, p. 1092.

Often this *is* justice. But far more frequently the Bible speaks of justice in terms of mercy, of loving-kindness, of unmerited care.

What is justice? Justice is simple fairness: The wrong-doers are punished and the victims are helped. Justice, therefore, is love carried out. Justice is caring for and serving. Justice is like peace: It ought not only to correct a wrong but also to be a state or atmosphere of well-being for all.

This definition, although valid, often does not go far enough. Simple fairness imposed on institutions and structures with built-in bias and deep-seated though perhaps subtle prejudice often will not produce justice. Just as the pilot must overcorrect to either side to get back on course, justice may require stepping on the toes of the favored. Justice often must become aggressive fairness. It is the *aggressive* fairness of such things as legislation in general, court orders, affirmative action, quotas that often creates controversy and hostility.

While justice is fairness, righteousness is simply doing right, "full of right." Mercy goes beyond fairness to become compassion and the ministration of unmerited love. If justice flows out of love, mercy flows out of justice. These terms are not merely conceptual or rhetorical in Scripture; they have bread-and-butter, nuts-and-bolts, rubber-hitting-the-pavement reality. We are told specifically how to be just and merciful. We are, for instance, to care for the widow, the orphan, and the alien—a triad mentioned time and again in Scripture from Deuteronomy to James and 3 John. Counterparts of these people are the modern-day recipients of welfare checks, food stamps, Medicaid, and the lonely, frightened, and poor in spirit in our families and churches.

Terence Radigan's *The Winslow Boy*, a drama based on a true story just before World War I, is about a British lad who was accused of forging a check at the boarding school he attended. His father believed in him and fought the case by hiring Sir Robert, one of Britain's most famous barristers. It became a cause célèbre. Finally two years later Sir Robert won the case. He went to the boy's home afterward and talked to the boy's sister, Cathy.

"Was it clear, cold logic that made you weep at the verdict?" she asked.

"I wept today because right had been done," Sir Robert replied.

"Not justice?" she asked.

"No, not justice," he said. "It is easy to do justice, very hard to do right. Unfortunately, while the appeal of justice is intellectual, the appeal of right appears for some odd reason to induce tears in court."

Occasionally these traits came together in a single chapter, such as Deuteronomy 16:18–20, or triumphantly in a few words:

Because I delivered the poor who cried,
And the fatherless who had none to help him.
The blessing of him who was about to perish came upon
    me,
And I caused the widow's heart to sing for joy,
I put on righteousness, and it clothed me;
My justice was like a robe and a turban,
I was eyes to the blind, and feet to the lame."
I was a father to the poor,
And I searched out the cause of him whom I did not know.
                    [Job 29:12–16]

For the word of the LORD is upright;
And all his work is done in faithfulness.
He loves righteousness and justice;
The earth is full of the mercy of the LORD.
                    [Ps. 33:4–5]

Give justice to the weak and the fatherless;
Maintain the right of the afflicted and the destitute.

Rescue the weak and the needy;
Deliver them from the hand of the wicked.

[Ps. 82:3]

Thus says the LORD: Do justice and righteousness, and
deliver from the hand of the oppressor him who has
been robbed. And do no wrong to the alien, the fatherless, and the widow. [Jer. 22:3]

William Shakespeare poignantly expressed this con-
nection between mercy and justice in *The Merchant of
Venice* through the words of Portia:

The quality of mercy is not strain'd,
It droppeth as the gentle rain from heaven
Upon the place beneath. It is twice blest:
It blesseth him that gives, and him that takes.
'Tis mightiest in the mightiest; it becomes
The throned monarch better than his crown;
His sceptre shows the force of temporal power,
The attribute to awe and majesty,
Wherein doth sit the dread and fear of kings;
But mercy is above this scept'red sway,
It is enthroned in the hearts of kings,
It is an attribute to God himself;
And earthly power doth then show likest God's
When mercy seasons justice.[5]

Justice as Compassionate Love

To love is to give care. To give care is to serve. Love,
thus, is service. We all understand, though perhaps imper-
fectly, what it means to love our spouses, our children,
our parents, our brothers and sisters, our friends. The
parent who responds to the child's cry or cough in the

5. Act 4, scene 1.

night surely is serving the tot—and loving the child. The one who befriends another, with no price or expectation attached, is loving and serving that person. Love is power.

Paul B. Henry said it this way: "It is justice which enables us to be the servants of both power and love."[6]

One of the greatest recorded love stories is that of Hosea and Gomer. God told Hosea to marry a prostitute, and because he was obedient, he did. She persisted in her evil ways. She left home to pursue her profession and fell into degradation. Finding her, Hosea bought her and took her home. The Lord told him to tell her: "I will betroth you to me in righteousness and in justice, in steadfast love, and in mercy" (Hos. 2:19). Righteousness, justice, mercy, love—all are part and parcel of each other, none enduring without the others.

Justice—Loving Those We Do Not Know

We do not readily grasp what it means to love people with whom we have only occasional contacts, those living in our cities in far different kinds of neighborhoods from where we live, those we never will meet, those living in the Third World who are as foreign to us as a Canaanite in a Bible story. But we must love them, too. To love those we do not know and who are beyond our sphere of personal contact is to seek to assure that justice and mercy are administered to them.

If we contend that we need love only those people with whom our lives directly intersect, we are trying to duck our responsibility for the other 99.99999 percent of the world's people, hardly what Christ intended in his admonition that we love others.

"The world is my parish," John Wesley said. Seneca, a Roman philosopher and political leader who lived con-

6. Henry, "Love, Power and Justice," p. 1090.

temporaneously with Christ, had an eloquent view of equality and a profound grasp of sin. He said, "I will look upon the whole world as my country. . . ." If we understand Christ's command to love one another (John 15:12) as including loving everyone in our world, we soon perceive that it is impossible directly to love all of them through personal acts. Then we discover that we can promote justice in a corporate way. One means is through Christian organizations; another is as a nation.

Justice—Goal of Politics, Duty of Government

Since we cannot love everyone personally and individually, we can love them through acts of justice carried out by government. Government is the only institution that is the corporate extension of us all, and thus it is our logical agent in administering justice.

My contention here is not intended to be partisan. I do not argue that big government is the key to social and economic justice. I simply assert that any party, Democratic or Republican, and any system, capitalism or socialism, must be judged by the criterion of justice. Always the powerful and those in authority must ask: What is truly just; what is truly right? These questions often are missing when political acts as well as personal behavior are measured.

Charles W. Colson was reflecting on this to me on the tenth anniversary of the Watergate break-in.

"Another reason I'm grateful for the whole Watergate experience is [now I have] a wholly different perception of justice, perhaps the most fundamental value of civil rights in a society. Certainly the glue that holds a civilization together is its concept of justice."

The remark came near the conclusion of a telephone interview. He began to speak with more passion than any time during the twenty-minute conversation.

When I was in the White House, justice to me was 50 percent of the vote plus one. Justice to me, when I was practicing law, was a client who paid me $100,000 a year to rewrite the law. To a kid growing up in the Depression seeing bread lines and my dad make thirty dollars a week, justice was protecting my property, getting my fair share. [Later] it was putting in prison people who couldn't obey the laws I made.

From prison I saw justice in a totally different way—from the standpoint of people who are forgotten in a society. Many of them don't know why they are there. Nobody cares about justice, in terms of guards being brutal, living in pits. I think I saw justice—just a glimpse—maybe Micah, Amos, Jeremiah and really the way God sees it. I've come to see man gets an inverted view of justice, the basic value in our society—what is right and what is important. I don't think my perception of justice will ever be the same again. I think I see it through the eyes of a God whose heart must break over the oppression of people. The more I study Scripture the more convinced I am God judges a society the way we treat the least, not the most powerful, a special place for the oppressed. I had to be there to feel that. I could never have intellectualized it. I had to be part of it.

Contrast Colson's words, spoken extemporaneously, with the picture of our society painted by Garry Trudeau, the Pulitzer Prize winning "Doonesbury" cartoonist.

"This is a deeply cynical age where generosity is in short supply," Trudeau said. "You will find this technological society will soon reveal its limitations. It is a world where taking a stand has come to mean finding the nearest trap door for escape. You will find . . . that your worth is measured not by what you are but by how you are perceived. There is something disturbing in our society where 'men wish not to be esteemed but to be envied.'" He condemned the television program *Saturday*

Night Live and its slash-and-burn humor, "where the
lame, the weak, the infirm, blacks, and women are the
easy targets of those who will place themselves above the
rest of us. The comedians reflect a society that is intoler-
ant of failure and short on compassion. If they are right,
all is lost."[7]

Trudeau may be a realistic satirist in portraying the
world. But all is not lost. We are called as a nation and
as individuals to perform the act of justice; indeed,
whether we do perform that act of justice will be the criterion by which we ourselves are judged.

If power is the means by which government works,
justice is, or ought to be, the goal of government.
President Jimmy Carter frequently said his number one
responsibility as chief executive was to protect the
national security. Ed McAteer, head of the Religious
Roundtable and a leader of the New Right, said
America's founding fathers established government "for
the purpose solely of restraining evil and protecting its
citizens."[8] But Carter and McAteer were only partly right.
I agree with what Reinhold Niebuhr has written, that the
sad duty of politics is to establish justice in a sinful
world.[9] Colson has said that one judges a nation by how
it treats the lower persons of society, not the highest.[10]

I have on occasion asked a politician who professes to
be a committed Christian by what yardstick God will judge
the United States or what are the marks of a Christian
nation, and I have seen that politician squirm and stutter.
Some Christians are more emphatic. They date America's
troubles to the 1973 Supreme Court decision legalizing

7. Garry Trudeau, commencement address at Colby College, Waterville,
Me., May 28, 1981. The "esteemed . . . envied" quotation was credited to historian Christopher Lasch.
8. Testimony to Senate Judiciary Committee, July 29, 1982.
9. Reinhold Niebuhr, *On Politics* (New York: Scribner's, 1960), p. 180.
10. Testimony to the House Judiciary Subcommittee on Penal Reform.

abortion and the 1962 Supreme Court decisions outlawing prayer in public schools. It may be that the killing of 1.5 million lives in the United States each year through abortions is the premier moral issue of the century, and it may be appropriate and even beneficial to allow a child to mouth a prayer in the classroom. But the Bible's definition of justice and righteousness and mercy goes far beyond that. Jamie Buckingham has observed, "Pro-life must mean more than anti-abortion."[11]

One of the most creative ways of administering justice in recent years involved a remarkable program the federal government began in the area of juvenile justice. At its core was the concept of restitution. The concept had its origin in the Hebrew testament, early in the days of the Israelite people. God told Moses while elaborating on the Ten Commandments that if a man stole an ox or a sheep, "he shall make restitution for it" (Exod. 22:3).

Under the program, begun in 1979 in twenty-six states, juveniles who committed crimes were not sent to prison or reform school but were ordered by the judges to make restitution to the people they had harmed. The results were nothing short of incredible. The success rate—that is, juvenile offenders who made full restitution and got into no more trouble while doing so—was more than 90 percent for first-time offenders. Even more astonishing was the success rate for juveniles who had committed very serious crimes or had five or more previous offenses: over 80 percent. Early data revealed that the victims recovered 87 percent of their losses. The benefits were enormous. The government was saved the $24,000 a year it costs to incarcerate a juvenile. The oft-ignored victims were recompensed. And young lives were changed.[12]

11. Letters, *Charisma*, October 1990, p. 14.
12. Oversight hearings on juvenile restitution programs, the House Education and Labor Committee's Human Resources Subcommittee, March 3, 1981.

At the very least, Christians can perform the act of justice to our nation and the world by serving as a conscience. When I pray, I try to avoid the ambiguous, innocuous prayer offering thanks for leaders who are born again and asking wisdom for them. I ask rather that they might be acutely sensitive to the biblical demands on them to seek justice and mercy and peace for the land.

Just off the rotunda on the second floor of the Capitol is a small room, the prayer room, established by an act of Congress. While on Capitol Hill I went there frequently. It did not encourage me to learn that of the 535 members of Congress and the 10,000 staff members about 10 persons visit it daily. The members of Congress may pray elsewhere—or they may not. On the other hand, about 200 or 300 persons attend the congressional staff prayer breakfasts, but rarely have I heard any discussion at those meetings of how the powerful in a nation ought to lead it toward justice and mercy.

The New Religious Right may properly pursue one or two passions, such as antiabortion and antipornography positions. But Christian people must see the gospel in its entirety. Others, fickle, may merely pause by poverty, racism, sexism, homelessness, drawn by whatever is currently chic. But what the Bible demands is that any system, any leader, any person, must be motivated to serve everyone justly and mercifully always.

In the Book of Ecclesiastes the writer, with an almost resigned attitude, says, "If you see in a province the poor oppressed and justice and right violently taken away, do not be amazed at the matter" (5:8).

During the turbulent years of the late sixties, I chaired the urban strategies task force at my church, Foundry United Methodist, in downtown Washington, D. C. We sponsored a preschool for neighborhood children; we cosponsored a community center; we hired an on-the-street community counselor; and we negotiated housing projects. At the same time, I was teaching Sunday school classes on the life of Christ and on the Holy Spirit. I was dismayed to see few persons who were working in our urban projects in my classes; I was even more dismayed to see few persons from those classes involved in our inner city projects. Both were wrong. Both saw a skewed gospel. Biblical truth comes alive through both Bible study and immersion in social justice.

Many of the activists of the sixties who now are working capitalists are proof of this. It is not that they were not speaking truth then; they often were. It is rather that by not pursuing the righteousness element in justice, they went dry and abandoned their causes.

Oswald Chambers said, "If I am devoted to the cause of humanity only, I will soon be exhausted and come to the place where my love will falter; but if I love Jesus Christ personally and passionately, I can serve humanity though men treat me as a door-mat."[13]

---

13. Oswald Chambers, *My Utmost for His Highest* (New York: Dodd, Mead, 1935), entry for June 19.

Case Study
The Carter White House

During my first week as a UPI reporter assigned to the White House in May 1975, while Gerald Ford was president, a crisis occurred. The Cambodians seized the American merchant ship *Mayaguez* en route from Hong Kong to Thailand. Within forty-eight hours President Ford sent in the Marines. In the exercise to retake the *Mayaguez* and in related exercises, thirty-seven American lives were lost—only one fewer than the number of crewmen saved on the ship.

The whole incident is highlighted in Ford's presidential library in Grand Rapids, Michigan, as one of the significant events of his presidency. Ford said his use of force provided "a firm assurance that the United States is capable and has the will to act in emergencies, in challenges."[1]

The next year, Jimmy Carter was elected president. I covered him daily from the time he had clinched the Democratic nomination in June 1976, until January 21, 1981, when immediately after he left office, we flew to Weisbaden, Germany, to welcome back the American hostages from Iran.

All of the hostages returned alive. But the perception of Carter as inept in dealing with the crisis was considered the most immediate cause of his defeat by Ronald Reagan. Inept or not, Carter's handling of the crisis was typical of the way he viewed the exercise of power. He used his power with great restraint.

1. *Weekly Compilation of Presidential Documents*, Vol. 11, No. 21, 1975, p. 515.

Throughout the short four years of his presidency, Carter's foreign policy was marked by several things: an emphasis on human rights, a reluctance to commit American troops to combat, and a refusal to use force to free the American hostages in Tehran.

It is my contention that his administration can be examined as a case study of the right use of power. He saw power as restraint in the use of force and as servanthood in the pursuit of justice.

The Source

Carter's basic beliefs grew from his studying the Bible on a daily basis and teaching Sunday school in the Baptist church almost weekly. My own systematic compilation and study of his religious remarks indicated an almost total reliance on the depth and breadth of Scripture, and not on studying Reinhold Niebuhr and other theologians as some writers have suggested. He quoted them comparatively infrequently.[2]

Carter was spiritually disciplined. He said often that he and his wife Rosalynn read the Bible together daily, without fail. He told me that he prayed many times during the day, "almost like breathing."[3] His speech was clean. He drank so little as to be nearly a teetotaler; the White House did not serve hard liquor during his administration. He gave nearly a tithe to his church. He attributed his passion for human rights to Scripture, saying "I've been steeped in the Bible since early childhood."[4]

2. Wesley G. Pippert, *The Spiritual Journey of Jimmy Carter* (New York: Macmillan, 1978).
3. Ibid., pp. 39–40.
4. Address to the General Council of the World Jewish Congress, Washington, D.C., November 2, 1977. This quotation and all subsequent others during Carter's years in office may be found in chronological order in *Public Papers of the President, Jimmy Carter* (Washington, D.C.: Government Printing Office).

Power as Restraint in Use of Force

Carter, by training and profession, was a military man. He was a graduate of the United States Naval Academy and had served as a naval officer for ten years. This made his views on the use of force all the more astonishing.

Paradoxically, Carter was not a pacifist in the sense of wanting to disarm America. He boasted frequently that during his administration he had reversed an eight-year trend of cutting real spending on defense and in fact had increased it every year. He claimed credit for the long-range missile program, a new tank, and a modern armored vehicle to carry fighting personnel. He also claimed credit for reversing a downward trend in purchases of Army equipment and jet fighter-attack aircraft. At one point he said: "Our ability to keep our nation at peace depends on our strength, our known strength. We've not only got to be strong, but the American people have got to know we're strong, our allies have got to know we're strong, and our potential adversaries have to know we're strong."[5]

Carter pointed out frequently that every day there are trouble spots in the world that might explode into combat. He mentioned that that had occurred during the time of his watch—Korea, Ecuador, Cuba, the Middle East, Pakistan, Angola. But he became the first president in fifty years, since Herbert Hoover, not to suffer the loss of American lives in combat.

This resolve was tested severely all during 1980. On November 4 the Iranians had taken over the United States Embassy in Tehran and captured embassy personnel. They remained hostage until the hour Carter left office January 21, 1981.

He never resorted to force. He continued to rely on other

5. Question-and-answer session, Addison, Ill., October 6, 1980.

methods: breaking off diplomatic relations, freezing Iranian assets in the United States, cracking down on Iranian students illegally in the United States, but never force. Some cite the helicopter crash in an Iranian desert during an abortive rescue mission in April 1980 as a combat loss of lives. But the lives were not lost to enemy gunfire.

During his unsuccessful 1980 campaign for reelection Carter returned again and again to his fundamental belief that power is to be used to serve and not to be used as force. The campaign proved to be a little-noticed forum in which he analyzed *why* this is true. In almost every case, Carter was speaking extemporaneously and not from a prepared text, indicating that his remarks reflected his personal feeling and not that of a speechwriter.

The following remarks are listed chronologically so as to demonstrate the progression in his mind of his analysis of power. Bear in mind, as well, that the remarks were made at a time the Americans had been held hostage for many months with no sign of any break.

The best weapons are the ones that are never used in combat, and the best soldier is the one who never sheds his blood on the battlefield. The best way to avoid combat that could kill tens of millions of Americans is for us to be strong and sure about our strength, but also that the president in the White House uses sound judgment and insists upon the maintenance of peace.[6]

It's always difficult for a powerful nation to be patient and not to capitalize in a political way over a tragedy like the capture of our innocent hostages.[7]

If you've got a strong military and you're jingoistic in spirit—that is, you want to push everybody around and

6. Interview with KOMO-TV, Tacoma, Wash., September 23, 1980.
7. Town Meeting, Flint, Mich., October 1, 1980.

just show the macho of the United States—that is an excellent way to lead our country toward war.[8]

It's a sign of weakness if you have to get involved militarily in a combat. It's a sign of strength if you can protect our nation's interests peacefully.[9]

A sign of strength of a country is when with calm assurance we can protect our national interest without using American military forces.[10]

I have always tried to use America's strength with great caution and care and tolerance and thoughtfulness and prayer, because once we inject our military forces into combat, as happened in Vietnam, it's hard to control it from then on, because your country loses prestige if you don't ultimately go ahead and win.[11]

Carter's remarks indicated these principles:

Power is to be used primarily to serve.
The possession of power often can lead to a macho, jingoistic attitude, the precursor of the use of force.
When power is used as force, it leads to the desire to use it to win and conquer.

Principle is reason enough to use force only with great restraint and as a last resort. But there proved to be a pragmatic value as well. Ford used force in seizing the *Maya-guez*—and almost as many lives were lost as were saved. Carter did not use force to get release of the hostages, and every one returned alive.

8. Addison, October 6, 1980.
9. Town Meeting, Nashville, Tenn., October 9, 1980.
10. Meeting with labor leaders, Secaucus, N.J., October 15, 1980.
11. Town Meeting, Pittsburgh, Pa., October 29, 1980.

"First Servant": The Pursuit of Justice

Jimmy Carter was from the South, a region long known for its overt racism and resistance to civil rights and its entrenched conservative chairmen in Congress. This made his views and policies all the more surprising. The tip, however, came early.

In general, the powerful and the influential in our society shape the laws and have a great influence on the legislature or the Congress. This creates a reluctance to change, because the powerful and the influential have carved out for themselves or have inherited a privileged position in society of wealth or social prominence or higher education or opportunity.[12]

In a speech before he became president, Jimmy Carter said:

Nowhere in the Constitution of the United States or the Declaration of Independence, nor the Bill of Rights, nor the Old Testament, nor the New Testament, do you find the words *economy* or *efficiency*. However, you find other words much more important—words like *self-reliance*, words like *beauty*, and words like *appreciation*, and words like *foresight*, and words like *stewardship*, *brotherhood*, *tenacity*, *commitment*, *compassion*, and *love*, that describe what a human being ought to be and also describe what the government of those human beings ought to be.[13]

He talked about why the powerful need restraints: "When you have complete freedom, the rich and the powerful overwhelm the poor and the weak."[14]

12. Address on Law Day, University of Georgia, May 4, 1974. See Pippert, *Spiritual Journey of Jimmy Carter*, pp. 96–97.
13. Address to National Wildlife Federation, Pittsburgh, March 15, 1975, ibid., 90.
14. Mexican Independence Day Rally, Saginaw, Michigan, September 16, 1976, ibid., 97.

In his remarks at the National Prayer Breakfast in Washington soon after he took office, Carter looked out at the vast gathering of the elite and powerful of Washington and said: "When the disciples struggled among themselves for superiority in God's eyes, Jesus said, 'Whosoever would be chief among you, let him be his servant.' And although we use the phrase—sometimes glibly—'public servant,' it's hard for us to translate the concept of a president of the United States into genuine servant."[15]

A few days later, during one of the traditional visits to the Cabinet departments that a new president makes, Carter told a group of government employees in a crowded, steamy cafeteria: "I need you to help me. We're all in it together. I'm no better than any of you. I recognize that I ought to be not First Boss but First Servant."[16]

These were not idle words. His interpretation of servanthood and justice took the form of civil rights and human rights. Take, for instance, minority appointments. A few days after his election Carter told reporters he would name more minority persons because of their historical exclusion from the mainstream. Statistics tell the story. Of his 1,195 full-time presidential appointments, 12 percent were women, 12 percent black and 4 percent Hispanic. Of a total 2,814 appointments, 23 percent were women, 12 percent black and 6 percent Hispanic. No other president ever approached these figures.

Carter attributed his passion for human rights to Scripture. "In large measure, the beginnings of the modern concept of human rights go back to the laws and the prophets of the Judeo-Christian tradition."[17] He expanded

15. National Prayer Breakfast, Washington, D.C., January 27, 1977.
16. To employees of the old Department of Health, Education and Welfare, Washington, D.C., February 16, 1977.
17. Address to the General Council of the World Jewish Congress, Washington, D.C., November 2, 1977.

the historic definition of human rights, which says it is the right to vote and not to be imprisoned without being charged. In a speech at the United Nations he said human rights also includes "the right of someone to have a place to work and a place to live and an education and an absence of disease, and, perhaps, an alleviation of hunger."[18]

Some experts questioned whether his emphasis on human rights had any effect. During his tenure, however, the Dominican Republic, Ecuador, Peru, and Brazil took significant steps away from totalitarianism toward majority rule. Probably every national leader in the world was compelled to become aware of human rights, perhaps Carter's main legacy. The future may reveal a relationship between Carter's emphasis on human rights and the wave of freedom that swept China and Eastern Europe in late 1989 and early 1990.

Greatness

In his farewell turn as teacher of the adult Sunday school class at the First Baptist Church in Washington in his waning days as president, Jimmy Carter spoke about greatness: "One of the things that Jesus teaches is, what is greatness? Is greatness being president? An emperor? A senior executive in a corporation? A very prominent, highly known news reporter or commentator? A powerful, behind-the-scenes manipulator of current events?"

Carter said instead Jesus teaches that "the foundation of greatness is service to others. The grasping for things that makes us look great in the eyes of other people is really a fruitless exercise. Quite often the richest people are the most unhappy, the most frustrated, have frequent

18. Remarks at a working luncheon for officials of Asian nations, October 5, 1977.

infidelity in marriages, despair and suicide. . . . The same thing happens with world leaders. The acquisition of power as measured in human terms is not greatness in the eyes of God."

The proof of his genuineness is, of course, that as a private citizen since leaving the presidency Carter has continued on a course of service to others, not on the aggrandizement of his wealth.

4

Authority and Leadership

All of us, the meek and the mighty, have power. But those who are in positions of leadership and authority possess a disproportionate amount of power. For most of us, our power is expressed in personal, individual ways. But persons in leadership and authority wield their power in ways that have vast implications for all of us.

Thus we must look carefully at these roles. Remarkably, we find that the characteristics of effective leadership and authority apply in very similar ways to the highest ranking officials in our land, to the heads of Christian organizations—or even to shop foremen or office managers.

We must distinguish between authority and leadership. Authority is power delegated to a person or an agency to carry out a particular task: the New York Port Authority, the schoolchild on patrol at the crossing, the Chicago

119

Transit Authority. None of these is to be equated with leadership, however; in fact, rarely does a person in authority become an authentic leader.

The leader transcends authority. A leader has contagious vision.

For instance, it is *not* necessary that a leader be a good administrator or manager. In these days of putting a premium on goal orientation and management skills and statistics gathering, we often err by equating effective administration with leadership. They are not the same, but we see the error propagated again and again. In the early days after the Exodus, Jethro, Moses' father-in-law, wisely knew that Moses was trying to do too much. "You will wear yourself out," Jethro said (Exod. 18:18). So Jethro suggested that Moses appoint judges and rulers to take some of the administrative burden. Jethro knew the difference between a manager and a leader.

Harvard's John Kotter has observed that good ideas are rarely lacking inside even poorly performing firms. The problem, he said, "is that the people who have the ideas can't get them implemented."[1] In other words, the ideas fail for want of effective leadership.

Consider the example of an eleemosynary organization. A charismatic person with a vision begins a movement, and it takes root, grows, and flourishes. Eventually the visionary leader dies or retires, and inevitably the organization decides, "We have been lacking in administration, so for our next president or chairman we need to select a good administrator." A good administrator is hired to shape up the organization, it starts to run like clockwork, and as often happens, the vision is lost.

Who remembers if Abraham Lincoln was a good

1. John P. Kotter, *Power and Influence* (New York: Macmillan's Free Press, 1985), pp. 8–9.

administrator? Or Franklin D. Roosevelt? And who
cares? Each had a vision that implanted him in history.
Today, it is not the Billy Graham organization's great
administrative skills, as awesome as they are, that make
Graham the great leader that he is.

Bill Bright had a vision that resulted in the founding of
Campus Crusade for Christ in 1951. Steve Douglass, Bruce
Cook, and two others did their master's research project at
the Harvard Business School in 1969 on how to organize
and structure Campus Crusade to accomplish Bright's
vision. At the time, Campus Crusade had 1,350 staff members. The four presented their thesis to Bright in a formal
ceremony. "Boy, this is great," Bright exclaimed. "We need
to do this. But who is going to do it?" So Douglass and
Cook volunteered to join Campus Crusade staff. Douglass
took on the role of director of planning and director of
management training, using the thesis as guidebook,
and four years later, he became vice president for administration. Campus Crusade today has a full-time staff of
10,000 and associate staff and trained volunteers number-
ing another 10,000. It has become one of the world's great
evangelistic movements on the strength of Bright's vision
and Douglass' managerial genius.

The great leader can employ a talented person to handle administrative details. But it is impossible to hire a
vision.

These were the attributes that the Fellows of Harvard
University said they were looking for in the search for a
new president: "He or she should surely have a distinguished intellect and recognized scholarly attainment.
The President must have strong leadership abilities,
excellent judgment with respect to people and to situations, ease with making decisions, many of which are
very difficult, and a developed understanding of management. Concern for Harvard in particular and higher edu-

cation more generally, and the courage to defend them, are important qualities. The individual should have imagination and vision and the eloquence to express them to the University and to the world."[2]

Sources of Authority

The nature of a person's authority is derived from the way that authority is bestowed, and may or may not depend on the person's proven ability. The following discussion outlines the most common sources of authority.

Democratic Election

In a democracy or republic the people hold the power and delegate their authority to the president and the legislators through elections.

An adjunct to this kind of authority is appointed authority. It is impossible to elect every single person in authority, so frequently the voters elect a person who then names a cabinet or department heads or committee chairmen, whether in government or in a smaller organization.

Israel, where I was a foreign correspondent for three years, has one of the purest democracies in the world. Each political party gets the same proportion of seats in the Knesset, the Israeli legislature, as it got in the election. Thus, a small movement can organize, poll 5 percent of the vote, and capture six seats in the 120-member Knesset. American-born Rabbi Meir Kahane, who advocated expulsion of the Arabs from Israel, was able to win a seat in the Knesset in 1984 by getting a small fraction of the vote. This means there are frequently fifteen or sixteen parties represented in the Knesset.

The party organizations themselves decide whose names

2. Letter to alumni, October 15, 1990.

are placed on their ballot and rank them. Israel's two major parties, the centrist Labor party and the right-wing Likud, generally elect thirty-five or forty members. The old-time party leaders are ranked at the top, 1-2-3-4, etc., thus assuring their certain election to the Knesset. This means, of course, that the top persons in both major parties keep getting elected to the Knesset and keep control of the leadership. While I was in Israel, three of modern Israel's eight prime ministers and a former president were serving in the coalition cabinet. In fact, in 1985, Shimon Peres was prime minister and Yitzhak Rabin was defense minister; a decade earlier, Rabin was prime minister and Peres was defense minister.

In the United States, it is winner take all. A presidential candidate can get 49 percent of the vote and lose out altogether. He does not get to continue in Congress as a leading member of the opposition. Meanwhile, the elected president can lose support in Congress and even of the people and still remain in office. In the United States, a new person lacking much Washington experience can emerge on the political scene and sweep through the primaries and win the presidency. This happened in the cases of Ronald Reagan in 1980 and Jimmy Carter in 1976. Neither could have become prime minister in Israel. On the other hand, only Lyndon B. Johnson and Gerald Ford, both of whom rose to congressional leadership posts, and George Bush have had anything like the experience that Israeli prime ministers have had.

In short, Israel's system assures that its leaders are always experienced, whereas the United States' system allows for the emergence of a new idea and a new vision. Both are democracies. But I prefer the American way, because it allows for new blood, new ideas, new possibilities.

One of the risks of a democracy is the great unevenness

in the competence and courage of chosen leaders. The ability to be persuasive with the electorate is not the same as the ability to be a visionary and to rule wisely. Certainly American presidents have not all been of the same quality. Vaclav Havel articulated some of the flaws of the Western democratic processes. Traditional parliamentary democracies are unable to deal with the automatism of technological civilization and the industrial-consumer society; in fact, he says, "people are manipulated in ways that are infinitely more subtle and refined than the brutal methods used in the post-totalitarian societies."[3] We have seen this in America, to cite one small example, in the increasing manipulation of the voters by political candidates through subtle, subliminal TV ads.

Inheritance

Some leaders inherit their authority. The monarchies of old are examples of inherited political authority. The subsequent generations of Rockefellers, Kennedys, and others are an example of inherited financial power. In many ways inherited leadership is the most perilous. Genes are no guarantee that the sons will be the equals of their fathers; look at the wise Solomon and the righteous Hezekiah and Joash and their evil sons.

My professor of Old Testament studies, the late J. Barton Payne, used to speak of "shirtsleeves to shirtsleeves in three generations: The first generation makes it, the second generation enjoys it, and the third generation squanders it. Back to shirtsleeves." The classic biblical reference to this, of course, is David, Solomon, and Jeroboam-Rehoboam. David solidified ancient Israel, Solomon enjoyed its early splendor, but the hostile broth-

---

3. Vaclav Havel, "The Power of the Powerless," in *Living in Truth*, ed. Jan Vladislav (London: Faber and Faber, 1987), p. 116.

ers Jeroboam and Rehoboam split the kingdom. Think of eminent families in our modern world. Rare indeed is the family in which the third generation still has the same inspiration and determination as the founding father.

Families depend on inherited authority. We did not elect our parents; we inherited them. We not only inherit our parents' genes, we also can inherit effects of emotional trauma they had as children, or effects of trauma they in turn might have inherited from our grandparents. Mere Christian belief is not enough to assure good parenting. The Old Testament records few instances of relationships between the righteousness of the father and the righteousness of the son or vice versa. As a comparatively new father, I realize how much I shape my children, and I also realize how little I can do to protect them from other forces. I'm not sure which scares me more.

Many of the problems that are endemic to inherited authority in families and political institutions are alike. Seeds sown early can bear bitter fruit. "The declining years of great empires seem to present an inevitability reminiscent of the last years of old people," said Sir John Glubb.[4] The forward-looking Abdul Hameed of the Ottoman Empire in the early 1900s inherited an aging, bureaucracy-bound empire that was on the brink of death; and indeed it did die in 1918.

Yet inherited authority has some marks of distinction that compel us to respect it. This was God's design. Perhaps the orderliness with which authority is passed on is one reason he chose this method of fashioning families.

Charisma

Perhaps the most effective—I do not say best but most effective—way of obtaining authority is the tribal method,

---

4. Sir John Glubb, *A Short History of the Arab Peoples* (New York: Stein and Day, 1970), p. 252.

in which one person emerges to the top exclusively by his or her wit or skill.

In the tribe the courageous man often became the leader, or the tribal chief derived his leadership directly from his heroic acts and his charisma.

Such were the "mighty men of valor" who appeared often in ancient Israel. The classic biblical examples were the judges. They usually had no pedigree and their behavior frequently was despicable. Gideon was a polygamist and entertained prostitutes. Jephthah was the son of a prostitute. Samson disregarded his parents' counsel in taking a Philistine wife and went to a prostitute. Gideon, Eli, and Samuel were poor parents who could not control their children. Yet the spirit of God had come on them, and despite their flaws they delivered Israel.

The term *charismatic* is drawn from the Greek word for grace. It probably was first used in recent American history to apply to John F. Kennedy; it unfortunately now has become a cliché. Max Weber, the German economist and sociological theorist of the early twentieth century, defined the charismatic leader as one set apart from the traditional, one endowed with exceptional qualities. "The term 'charisma' will be applied to a certain quality of an individual personality by virtue of which he is set apart from ordinary men and treated as endowed with supernatural, superhuman, or at least specifically exceptional powers or qualities."[5]

Of the various kinds of persons in authority, the charismatic comes closest to being an authentic leader.

5. Max Weber, *The Theory of Social and Economic Organization*, trans. A. M. Henderson and Talcott Parson (New York: Oxford University Press, 1947), pp. 358–392 for full discussion.

Qualities of Leadership

We find little to do with management, administration, campaigning and elections, or public relations in defining the leader. What are the marks of effective leadership?

Vision

"Where there is no vision, the people perish," Solomon said (Prov. 29:18 KJV). The foremost mark of a leader is that he or she has a vision. This is true whether the leader heads a nation, a corporation, a religious organization, or even a family. Vision is the garland that anoints authority with leadership.

Just before leaving office, while at dinner with a small group of us reporters, President Jimmy Carter reflected on his administration. He said he had found the National Security Council, directed by Zbigniew Brzezinski, much more innovative and creative than the State Department, which was hidebound by tradition and the proper way of doing things. Many of the diplomats in Foggy Bottom (Washington's nickname for the State Department) had reached their level in part by doing things in the accepted way. On the other hand, staffers in the NSC owed their loyalty to one man—the president—and not to the formal attire of the Foreign Service; hence, they were much more willing and likely to be daring and visionary.

Administrators and managers are skilled in the tactics and techniques of the institution (by definition institutions are structured tradition). Their very skill may become inhibiting. The leader often must break the mold and burst out of the usual manner of doing things. The leader must dream dreams.

In the early 1970s, Representative Wilbur D. Mills was considering a race for the presidency. Surely no one was more qualified. He was the longtime chairman of the

House Ways and Means Committee and one of the most powerful persons in Congress. During an appearance at the Washington Press Club he rattled off answers easily and knowledgeably. Finally I asked, "Chairman Mills, when you dream about America, what do you dream?"

Mills was taken aback. "Why," he said, "I could talk about that all night." But he could not or would not answer the question. And neither was he elected president. Knowing the intricacies of the tax code and how the government runs is not the same as leading a nation.

The Scriptures tell us far more about the prophets than about the kings of Judah and Israel. The kings may have headed the government, but the prophets had the vision. Perhaps the fatal flaw of all dynasties has been that mere heredity does not assure a ruler of vision. A person is not born with a vision; one must obtain it through conviction or circumstance.

Moses was old and he protested that he was not an orator, but God gave him a vision, and he led the Israelites out of Egypt. God gave Joshua a vision of the Promised Land, and he conquered Canaan. Many of the judges had checkered personal histories, and the record is sparse as to what kind of administrators they were. But God gave them the vision of saving the land from oppressors, and they did so.

Shortly before his retirement as dean of Wesley Seminary in Washington, D.C., I interviewed Harold DeWolf, who years before had been Martin Luther King, Jr.'s doctoral chairman at Boston University. Thinking of a story angle to hang DeWolf's observations on, I asked him whether he had any clue while King was a doctoral student as to the kind of leader he would become.

"I didn't know him very well," DeWolf replied. My first reaction was a bit of disappointment, but when he explained, my estimation of King as a leader only soared.

DeWolf said that most doctoral students really struggle —struggle over their work, their dissertations, their nonacademic lives. "Those I got to know very well," DeWolf said. "But Martin Luther King always knew exactly where he was headed. He would have his questions in order, he would come for his appointment with me, we would sail through them, and out the door he went. So I never got to know him very well." King had a clear vision.

King wrote that he sailed through his childhood and even graduate school with "no burdens." When he got to Montgomery, his vision took form and clashed with the world. He never was the same again. He wrote that he was ready to give up, and one night he took his problems to God over the kitchen table. "I am here taking a stand for what I think is right. I am afraid. The people are looking to me for leadership," he prayed. "At that moment I experienced the presence of God as never before." Shortly after, the Montgomery bus boycott was born.

Greenleaf suggests that a leader needs two intellectual abilities that are not usually formally assessed in an academic way: "a sense for the unknowable" and the ability to "foresee the unforeseeable."[6] These are not mere mystical or supernatural gifts, he says. Rather, they involve intuition, a "feel" for patterns, the ability to generalize on what has happened previously.

What happens to the family that has no vision? My mother, after the kitchen was clean and the children were in bed, would pray for her family until the wee hours. Late one night, she opened her Bible and the words, "I will save thy children" (Isa. 49:25) leaped out at her. She claimed that as a promise, and she saw the promise come true for every one of her children and every one of her many grandchildren. What was emphasized in our home was

---

6. Robert K. Greenleaf, *The Servant as Leader* (Cambridge, Mass.: Center for Applied Studies), pp. 14–15.

not making money but ministry and service to others, and nearly every one of the next two generations chose professions that were directly related to Christian ministry or professions that helped others.

The matter of vision is also important to us personally. I had wanted to become a reporter since I was in the sixth grade in a one-room country school. (In pondering this, I think I never presumed I could wield power politically, but being a reporter did allow me to observe it up close.) When I got to the University of Iowa, I met other Christians through Inter-Varsity Christian Fellowship, and my faith took on dimension. The academic side of this was a desire to know myself and others more closely, and I decided to pursue a doctorate in social psychology. I took a job as a correspondent with United Press, always intending to go on to study social psychology. I didn't, of course; I remained a reporter, and I'm glad I did. My settling on journalism indicated a restless curiosity, I suppose. Along the way I became a lay pastor for five years, went on an archaeological excavation in the Middle East, and was a political press spokesman. Even after I settled on being a reporter, I didn't stick to one beat or one location; instead, I went from covering state capitals to covering Washington D.C., and in Washington from covering Watergate to the White House to Congress. Then abruptly I became a foreign correspondent in the Middle East. Someone once remarked to me that if I had focused all my energy and attention on one thing from the start, I would have reached several higher levels of accomplishment. Being a curious person I often let my choices be dictated by opportunities that opened up, not on following a carefully designed plan.

To have one's sights clearly focused—to have a vision— often propels one to the lofty heights of leadership.

Courage

Two Arabs—the late Anwar Sadat, president of Egypt, and Yasser Arafat, chairman of the Palestine Liberation Organization—present starkly contrasting portrayals of courage. They both dealt with Israel, but in vastly different ways.

The Egyptian president's trip to Jerusalem in 1977 was the first significant breakthrough in the modern struggle between Israel and the Arab world. Israelis credit Sadat, not the Americans, with the breakthrough. Sadat persisted in his derring-do by going to Camp David in 1978 to negotiate with Israeli Prime Minister Menachem Begin and signing a peace treaty with Israel the following year. Sadat took the bold move with no support from other Arabs. He demonstrated that the great leader has courage. He paid for his vision and courage with his life—an assassination by brother Arabs.

I never covered Sadat, but I did cover Yasser Arafat. It was the fall of 1983, and Arafat, who has more lives than a cat, and the PLO were about to be driven out of Tripoli, Lebanon. Each day we foreign correspondents would rent a taxi—generally a white Mercedes—in Beirut and make the incredibly lovely drive up the rugged Mediterranean coastline to Tripoli. Our purpose was twofold: to see whether he was still in Tripoli, and whether he was still alive. While our driver opened the trunk of his Mercedes and made tea from an elegant miniature tea set, Arafat would drive up in a dusty car and go into a Spartan building in a wretchedly poor neighborhood for a news conference.

He was serene, jaunty, and impeccably dressed— peaked cap, black and white scarf tucked in his olive jacket—his straggly beard notwithstanding. He handled hostile questions easily, his smile never leaving his face. There was a charisma about him. One day a woman quickly made her way to him in the crowded room. She threw her arms around him and laid her head on his chest and sobbed. He put his hands gently on her face and looking into it said something softly. Then he kissed her forehead. A second woman did the same thing. A few minutes later two boys rushed up to him and started calling him by his nickname, Abu Amar, which is loosely translated "founding father." As if he had all the time in the world, he playfully showed them how to make V-for-victory signs with their fingers. Then he got in his dusty car and drove off.

An Arab diplomat put him into perspective for me. Arafat, he said, has an emotional need to work by consensus. He will do only what he feels his supporters, the various factions of the PLO, will support. Time and again Arafat has indicated he is willing to move toward tacitly recognizing Israel or at least halting violence, then backed off at the last minute. For an entire year, during 1985, he joined with Jordan's King Hussein to work on a joint Jordanian-Palestinian negotiating team. But he could not take the final step, and Hussein finally threw up his arms in disgust during a three-hour address, which I had the chore of helping cover.

Compare Arafat's need for consensus with Sadat's lonely daring. It is clear who had the courage, and thus, who accomplished peace.

Henry A. Kissinger, during a discussion of Sadat, captured this distinction:

> The difference between great and ordinary leaders is less formal intellect than insight and courage. The great man understands the essence of a problem; the ordinary leader grasps only the symptoms. The great man focuses on the relationship of events to each other; the ordinary man sees only a series of seemingly disconnected events. The great

man has a vision of the future that enables him to put obstacles in perspective; the ordinary leader turns pebbles in the road into boulders.[7]

I was afraid—afraid of girls, afraid of not being accepted, afraid of asking the wrong questions. During my university years, something came to me: I could acknowledge my fears—not deny them—but acknowledge them—and then go ahead and do whatever it was I feared. It was emancipating. One evening I was attending a production of Shakespeare's *Measure for Measure* at the Kennedy Center in Washington. There came Lucio's words, which stated what I had accepted as a credo:

Our doubts are traitors,
And makes us lose the good we oft might win
By fearing to attempt.[8]

Courage is not the denial of fear; it is the conquering of fear. It is to be seen in great leaders.

Ability to Inspire

The great leader must not only have a dream but must share it. The leader must be able to inspire the people and motivate them. The effective leader must make the vision contagious. Communication is the key.

The soaring words of Franklin D. Roosevelt and John F. Kennedy surely were responsible in part for the attractiveness of their leadership. King's 1963 "I have a dream" speech at the Lincoln Memorial in Washington, which became the theme of the civil rights movement of the 1960s, still arouses powerful emotions, not merely for the

---

7. Henry A. Kissinger, *Years of Upheaval* (Boston: Little, Brown, 1982), p. 647.
8. Act 1, scene 4.

meaning of his words but also because of the way he delivered them.

What guarantees an effective communicator? The knack of telling a good story? Old-fashioned rhetoric? Clarity and succinctness? The tone and modulation of the voice? Body language? We may answer, "All of these," or even "None of these."

Jimmy Carter's biggest failure as president, in my view, was his inability to communicate his vision for the nation and to inspire people. He had a vision: energy self-sufficiency for the nation, compassion for the minorities, human rights for the oppressed of the world. But he seldom could make his case effectively, and people denied his request for reelection.

Carter spoke, whether from texts or extemporaneously, in complete sentences, with subjects and verbs. The texts of his extemporaneous remarks read as well as those in a prepared speech. In delivery his words were often eloquent, but his tone lacked power. Often, in political or official speeches, he emphasized the wrong word, or ran phrases together and put pauses in the wrong places. I frequently saw people drift away from the edge of an outdoor crowd when he was speaking on the stump. The effect was deadly. With a couple of exceptions.

When Carter taught Sunday school or spoke to a black audience, the atmosphere became electric. There was a reason for this. He grew up in an overwhelmingly black hamlet, and his childhood was steeped in the Baptist church; among these people he felt at home. Once, during the 1976 campaign, he spoke to a group of black preachers, themselves master speakers. He talked about Jesus: "He walked the streets. . . . He touched blind eyes. . . . He healed those who were crippled. . . . He changed the lives of those who didn't go to church." At each of Carter's phrases, in this case precisely placed, the black preachers roared back, "Amen! . . . Preach it, brother! . . . Do it! Do it! . . . Hallelujah!"

His conqueror, Ronald Reagan, who was known as "the great communicator," spoke with a childlike innocence and winsomeness. He tilted his head back, smiled, and began, "Well. . . ." He projected being affable, genial, sincere, and a sort of "who? me?" look in response to any challenge. Reagan has had to project himself all his adult life as a sportscaster, actor, General Electric spokesman, politician. He was the master of the TelePrompTer and the prepared text. But the effect was often overwhelming.

Nowadays the old-fashioned orators—such as Douglas MacArthur and Winston Churchill—are gone. The late Senate Republican leader Everett McKinley Dirksen, whose voice sounded like a pipe organ, was king. With his word that it was "an idea whose time has come" ringing out, Dirksen, more than any other, was ultimately responsible for passage of the 1964 civil rights act. Hubert H. Humphrey rivaled him, and although his voice was high pitched and squeaky, he could speak endlessly and communicate boundless enthusiasm and joy on any subject.

Moses was so aware of the need for effective communication that he protested the Lord's call to lead the Israelites because he was "not eloquent . . . but . . . slow of speech and of tongue" (Exod. 4:10). God, as he often does, overruled Moses' weakness and summoned him to lead the nation anyway. But Moses was the exception, not the rule.

It is not merely tone, of course, but the power of the words as well that makes for effective communication. We cannot listen to Abraham Lincoln's voice, but reading his "Second Inaugural Address" at the Lincoln Memorial still moves people to tears. We do not know what kind of a voice David had, but his psalms demonstrate that his words were tremendously powerful and obviously played a huge part in his effectiveness. AFL-CIO President Lane Kirkland had a gravelly voice, but I saw grizzled reporters with tears running down their cheeks when Kirkland eulogized his predecessor, labor leader George Meany: "Now he is young and strong again, free of pain, blessed with a rich store of grace, starting over with the steadying, and when needs be, the humbling force of Eugenia," his wife who had died a few months earlier.[9]

English historian William Edward Hartpole Lecky, an expert on the evangelical revival of the 1700s, has given a classic description of George Whitefield as preacher:

> His preaching combined almost the highest perfection of acting with the most burning fervor of conviction. No man ever exhibited more wonderfully the strange power which great histrionic talent exercises over the human mind—investing words which are in truth the emptiest bombast with all the glow of the most majestic eloquence, and imparting, for the moment at least, to confident assertions more than the weight of the most convincing arguments. His gestures were faultless in their beauty and propriety, while his voice was so powerful that Franklin, who was the most accurate of men, ascertained by experiment that it could be heard distinctly in the open air by 30,000 persons. . . . Garrick is reported to have said, with a pardonable exaggeration, that Whitefield could pronounce the word *Mesopotamia* in such a way as to move an audience to tears.[10]

But far more is involved in the ability to inspire than mere rhetoric. Rhetoric in itself does not assure the presence of a vision. A politician can hire a stable of skilled

---

9. At funeral for Meany, St. Matthew's Cathedral, Washington, D.C., January 15, 1980.

10. Umphrey Lee, *The Lord's Horseman* (Nashville: Abingdon Press, 1928), p. 77.

wordcraftsmen to make speeches that sing and phrases that purr, the role that Peggy Noonan played for Ronald Reagan and in writing George Bush's acceptance speech at the 1988 Republican National Convention. But if the politician is hollow and devoid of a vision, all the words in the world cannot make that person a leader. In modern parlance, that person is "all style and no substance."

Skill in Resolving Conflicts

The leader also must be able to mesh and smooth the differing points of view of many people, frequently necessary in today's world.

This came to me vividly while I was chief UPI correspondent in Israel. My original staff was made up of one *sabra* (a native-born Israeli), one American Jew who had gone on *aliyah* (to Israel to live), two American Jews working on temporary assignment in Israel; and I, a Gentile. When one of the American Jews returned to the United States, we replaced him with a Palestinian. UPI was the first Western news agency to employ a Palestinian in a professional role in Israel. Think of leading that staff!

I wish I could say I succeeded. The Palestinian, only in his forties, had suffered the burden of being known among fellow Arabs as someone who worked with Jews, and he was known among Jews as an Arab. He slid to burnout and left the staff after a few months. But one scene sticks vividly in my mind.

Several of us sat in the spacious UPI bureau in the *Yedioth Ahrenot* newspaper building in Tel Aviv. I looked around the group. There were the Israeli *sabra*, the American Jew and I, all from my staff; a reporter from the German Press Agency (DPA); and a reporter from the Italian news agency (ANSA). I realized the significance of the makeup of the group, how much blood had been shed by our various countrymen fighting each other. But our conversation was easy and relaxed. Whatever our pasts, we were bound together by a common task—covering the news. A conflict of the ages had been quieted by a common purpose—at least for a few moments.

"Leading one hundred people who all have the same basic goals, values, and perspectives is one thing," Kotter says. "Heading a similar-sized group that is composed of twenty warring factions is something else completely."[11]

Conflict resolution does not involve forcing (there's that word again) a settlement on the differing parties. Manipulating the parties to settle a dispute can lead to loss of trust of each other and their leader.

I have often reflected on my experience as a bureau chief in the Middle East. A few things I did right. I had courage, often masking a lot of inner trembling. I moved the main UPI bureau from Tel Aviv to Jerusalem, despite fears it would alienate our Arab clients. I added a Palestinian to our staff. I tried to identify the skill of each staff member and then give that staffer as much opportunity as possible to use that unique skill in going after stories that fit that skill. I didn't hesitate to hand the biggest story of the month to a talented young intern when more senior members of the staff were floundering with it. And the youngster quickly began to clobber the opposition.

"Splendid Isolation"

But some things I did were not effective. I acted as too much a peer with the rest of the staff, not the leader apart. I did not articulate adequately my vision that we ought to pursue aggressively stories that dealt with issues of justice and peace (although our bureau wrote proba-

11. Kotter, *Power and Influence*, p. 38.

bly as many if not more such stories than any other news agency there).

Kotter speaks again and again of the importance for maintaining dialogue and good relationships with bosses, subordinates, subordinates of subordinates, peers in other parts of the organization, or as he put it simply, "friendships."[12] Nowadays the cliché for this is "networking." On the other hand, the charismatic person, the leader, is set apart from others. Harry Truman described the presidency as "splendid isolation." Or to put it another way, a plaque on Truman's desk said, "The buck stops here." Ultimately, the leader stands alone.

Authority (Again)

The leader must have not only a vision and the ability to communicate it but also the authority to carry it out.

The midtwentieth-century history of the United States has seen a teeter-totter exchange of authority between the president and Congress in running the nation. Theodore Roosevelt started the trend toward a strong presidency, but Franklin D. Roosevelt was the first of the modern chief executives to centralize the power of the federal government in the White House. At the start of World War II, the State, War, and Navy departments were housed in one building, a rococo structure next door to the White House.[13] Now the State Department is housed in a block-square building in Foggy Bottom, and the Defense Department already has spilled out of the biggest office building in the world, the Pentagon. The rococo building next to the White House contains merely the overflow office staff of the president.

12. Ibid.
13. For a fascinating description of the transition of Washington during World War II, see David Brinkley, *Washington Goes to War* (New York: Ballantine, 1988).

More important than this, the power of the president grew so much that Lyndon B. Johnson was able to conduct the war in Vietnam without a formal declaration of war by Congress as required by the Constitution. This led to passage of the 1973 War Powers Act, which requires the president to get congressional approval for keeping American forces abroad for more than a limited period. Richard Nixon was condemned for using far too much authority, Jimmy Carter for being unwilling to use enough.

In the United States, the two-term president has become the exception, not the rule as it was throughout the 1800s. In the twentieth century only four presidents have served two full terms: Wilson, F. D. Roosevelt, Eisenhower, and Reagan. This was because of an assassination and a resignation of two who might have served two full terms, and because some presidents were defeated for a second term (Hoover, Ford, and Carter) or withdrew because they knew they would be defeated if they ran again (Truman and Johnson).

Goodness: the Hero

The best leader has not only vision and charisma but also an essential goodness and decency.

On one of my first trips aboard Air Force One, President Ford was returning from Mackinac Island in his home state of Michigan. A press pool—a small group of reporters who accompany the president when space or other considerations cannot accommodate the entire White House press corps—sit in the aft of the plane, and presidents frequently stroll back to chat, generally on an off-the-record basis. This Sunday afternoon Ford came wandering back. He had been playing golf and was still in his knit shirt and slacks, a stubble on his chin. This was at a time when Ford, whose rise to fame came as House Republican leader, had been vetoing almost record numbers of bills. At one point I asked Ford if all those vetoes were hurting his long relationships on Capitol Hill.

"Nah," he said with a laugh. "Those vetoes are just politics. They don't have anything to do with my friendships." The remark struck me as that of a healthy and good man who had things in their proper perspective.

America has had too few heroes recently. Instead we have had the names of Ivan Boesky, Jim Bakker, Richard Nixon, fallen and fallible men. "God has relented and is giving us heroes, at least in other lands," wrote columnist Mary McGrory.[14] She was writing about Vaclav Havel, the Czech playwright who went from prison to the presidency in weeks, and Nelson Mandela, the South African black leader. She also could have cited Lech Walesa of Poland, F. W. de Klerk of South Africa, and Mikhail Gorbachev of the Soviet Union. Gorbachev won the Nobel Peace Prize in 1990.

My own personal hero was Pete Dawkins. Dawkins was the all-American halfback at West Point in 1958, and by 1981 the youngest general in the army. But Pete Dawkins was much, much more than that. He was the most luminous graduate ever produced by the U.S. Military Academy at West Point. There are several ways to win fame at West Point: as first captain of the cadet corps; as captain of the football team; as class president; as "star" man or woman, someone in the top 5 percent of the class. The nonpareil Douglas MacArthur was first captain and star man in 1903. Dawkins was *all* of those things. Nobody ever accomplished that before or since.

That wasn't all. Dawkins played a half-dozen musical instruments. He sang. He won the coveted Heisman football trophy to the outstanding collegiate player that year. He won a Rhodes scholarship to Oxford. He mastered

14. Universal Press Syndicate, February 25, 1990.

rugby. He won a doctorate at Princeton in international politics. He was disciplined. Nearly twenty-five years after his football exploits, he remained precisely at his midseason playing weight. He began playing the piano again in middle age.

In a conversation with me Dawkins spoke about heroes and how America needs them to personify and make real its virtues. What made his remarks all the more significant is that they were given spontaneously, indicating that they sprang from his deep beliefs and were not the result of an intellectual exercise.

"It's terribly important to have heroes. A lot of things that are really central parts of our lives are transcendent or abstract," Dawkins told me. "But it's hard for us to deal with courage or dedication or sacrifice in the abstract. We need to have people who embody those qualities, who are reassuring and real."

A good leader must be heroic, one who exemplifies qualities of goodness. Goodness surely includes the virtues of integrity, fidelity, decency, discipline.

The president of the United States is more than the chief executive, the head of state, the commander-in-chief, and the head of his party. He also is the symbolic leader of the people, by far his most important task. This is why I believe the press have not only the right but also the obligation to probe every aspect of his life. He is the parent figure for the country. He sets the tone not merely for the White House and his administration but also for the entire nation. The president must be a hero.

Three small examples leap to my mind in communicating the importance of the goodness of a leader and how the people mime that leader. People also mime less desirable traits. In one large newsroom in which I served, the news editor was a legendary journalist with brilliant writing ability, and he smoked Chesterfield cigarettes. A

fledgling reporter named Bill started work. He was un-
kempt, disheveled, and often was found sleeping at night
back in the storeroom. It was clear the news editor was
planning to dismiss him before his six-month probation-
ary period was up. One day, a colleague sidled up to the
news editor, who was quietly sitting in a bar eating lunch
and sipping his beer, and remarked, "Dave, have you
noticed that Bill has switched to Chesterfields?"

People mimic leaders; leaders ought to be worthy of
being mimicked. I was Senator Charles H. Percy's first
press aide in Washington. Percy lived a clean, disciplined
life, never swore, did not smoke, and drank only Dubonnet wine. At an office gathering, another member of the
staff whispered to me, "Do you notice that almost everyone is drinking Dubonnet?"

Some people tend to segregate public and private morality. We ought not to be too quick to do this. We are whole
people. What affects me in one area is bound to affect me
in another. The ancient Hebrews knew this; even a person's name reflected his character. Drew University sponsored a 1977 conference on the topic, "Private and Public
Ethics: Tensions Between Personal Integrity and Institutional Responsibility in American Life." David Little,
an ethicist at the University of Virginia and a participant, said, "It's impossible to divide public from private
morality in any neat, dichotomous way. . . . Any simplistic division or notion of two moralities will not wash."
Little's contention was echoed by virtually every other
participant.

I talk frequently to a man who is the editor of a liberal
magazine, a Democratic national committeeman, and
was a state chairman for the Carter campaign. This man
had experienced political difficulty with Hamilton Jordan,
who was Carter's top aide. He told me frankly that he was
convinced that Jordan's cavalier manner of dealing with a

political ally was related to his notorious personal antics. The liberal editor also remarked to me, "I used to say I didn't care what a senator did in off hours, all I cared was how he voted. I don't say that anymore." The editor had sensed correctly how our private and public lives are related.

The stories about the private lives of John F. Kennedy and Lyndon B. Johnson are rife—and ripe. I asked the late Peter Lisagor, White House correspondent for the *Chicago Daily News,* whether he heard of Kennedy's alleged womanizing while he was president. Lisagor, a top reporter who would have heard had there been such rumors, told me no. We must treat these women's ex post facto stories about their alleged romances with Kennedy with some skepticism. On the other hand, the same skepticism does not extend to tales about Edward M. Kennedy. If he were chief executive, White House wire service reporters would spend much of their time "staking out" the president, that is, watching him closely any time he was in public and watching the main White House gate to see who came and went.

Goodness ought to be an essential part of leadership. The decency of Gerald Ford, the purity of Jimmy Carter, and the affable nature of Ronald Reagan provided a healing light to "the long dark night," in Ford's phrase, of the Watergate scandal, and perhaps even the ruthlessness of Johnson and the inclination of Kennedy to bend the truth.

Another example of the relationship of personal goodness and public practice was a study funded by the National Endowment for the Humanities and conducted by a research team headed by Peter L. Benson. It revealed a "profound" relationship between religious beliefs and voting patterns in Congress. The team sent questionnaires to 112 selected members of Congress in 1979–80 and followed up by interviewing 72 of them. The study classified the members in six religious categories cutting across denominational lines: nominal, 22 percent; legalistic, emphasizing rigid rules and lifestyle, 15 percent; self-concerned, seeing religion as a source of personal comfort, 29 percent; people-concerned, with a marked concern for social justice, 10 percent; integrated, with a balance of religious themes, 14 percent; and nontraditional, who believe in a more abstract God, 9 percent.[15]

The researchers then examined those persons' voting records on civil liberties, foreign aid, abortion, government spending, military, school prayer, and market competition. They found that on every voting measure, the legalistic and self-concerned members of Congress were most conservative in votes on these issues and the people-concerned and nontraditional members were the most liberal.

"The evidence is strong that ties between religious world view and political decision making are profound," the study said.

Senate Chaplain Richard C. Halverson has said that one-half of all senators attend the weekly senate prayer breakfast occasionally, and a quarter of them do so regularly. What goes on during the breakfasts is not known publicly, but the assumption is that generally the breakfasts become times of close, personal fellowship. The senators speak of the value of their simply being a "Christian presence." Jacques Ellul has written that a Christian "is a 'sheep' not because his action or his sacrifice has a purifying effect on the world, but because he is the living and real 'sign,' constantly renewed in the midst of the world, of the sacrifice of the Lamb of God."[16]

This in itself does not assure the Christian legislator

15. Peter L. Benson, "God Is Alive in the U. S. Congress," *Psychology Today* 15/12 (Dec. 1981): 46–57.

16. Jacques Ellul, *The Presence of the Kingdom* (New York: Seabury, 1967), p. 11.

will be committed to justice and the good use of power, but it does help the legislator to be a good person.

The Old Testament judges were men and women on whom the spirit of the Lord had come. It is significant that the Israelites took a title—judge—that actually was derived from the concept of justice and elevated it to one of national leadership. The judges' duties as leaders of the nation included but went beyond being judicial officers. They saved Israel from oppression.

Fortunately history tends to remember the leader who is committed to justice more than the ruthless tyrant. Michael Hart's book *The 100: A Ranking of the Most Influential Persons in History*[17] includes the wicked as well as the saintly. It is no coincidence that every one of his top ten—Mohammed, Newton, Christ, Buddha, Confucius, St. Paul, Ts'ai Lun, Gutenberg, Columbus, and Einstein—was committed to doing the right thing. Those whose acts were evil or led to evil were few and far between. Marx, the formulator of communism, ranked eleventh. Lenin, Mao, Genghis Khan, Hitler, Stalin, and Machiavelli were about the only others on the list whose deeds were wrong.

Hitler, obviously, was an effective leader. Mussolini made the trains run on time. But it is not enough for a leader merely to be effective or influential. The good leader must be committed to justice and peace and the right use of power.

17. New York: Beaufort Books, 1985.

Case Study
Joseph and David

Joseph and David present remarkable profiles of leadership. Both were great and beloved of God. Joseph erred rarely; David was vastly human in ways that we are. Both used their positions of authority to promote justice among the people they served.

Joseph

The Book of Genesis (chapters 37–50) reveals inspiringly how young Joseph, an alien in a foreign land, braved the temptations of another culture, the advances of his superior's wife, and success, and emerged as a good leader.[1]

Joseph was a mere teenager when his jealous brothers dropped him into a pit at Dothan, a settlement in what is now the occupied West Bank. Traders carried him off to Egypt, and there he rose to become, in effect, Pharaoh's prime minister. It is one thing to become a leader among your own people; it is something else to become a leader in a foreign land. Today it would be akin to a Jew becoming prime minister of an Arab country.

On his upward journey Joseph resisted pride, sexual lust, arrogance—sins common to both prominent and not-so-prominent people with power.

"Handsome and good-looking" (as Genesis 39:6 des-

---

1. Thomas J. Barrett, who formerly spent much time on Capitol Hill for the Christian Embassy, has provided a helpful study of Joseph.

cribes him), Joseph resisted sexual temptation. "How then can I do this great wickedness and sin against God?" (39:9), he said in spurning his master's wife. He did not bank on his own willpower to resist but fled from her (imperative advice for anyone dealing with sexual temptation). How many people are willing to risk their jobs, as Joseph did, to resist temptation? Even though the angered woman saw to it that Joseph went to prison, he remained steadfast in his fidelity to God.

He did not hide his faith; his master "saw that the LORD was with him" (39:3). Joseph recognized that his ability came from God, for he told Pharaoh, "It is not in me; God will give Pharaoh a favorable answer" (41:16). Many persons in positions of power have fallen prey to pride. But even as "prime minister" during Egypt's long drought Joseph never lost sight of the greatness of God.

"Fear not, for am I in the place of God?" (50:19), he said many years later to his now fearful brothers. He refused to be bitter against them even when he had plenty of reason to be.

In the conclusion of the story, Joseph declared to his brothers the purpose behind everything that had happened to him: "As for you, you meant evil against me; but God meant it for good, to bring about that many people should be kept alive, as they are today" (50:20).

Joseph's faith helped him to be good. That principle still holds true today.

Joseph was also a contradiction. His father loved him (Gen. 37:4), and one can assume quite safely that his father's love contributed mightily to the strength of Joseph's character. Joseph knew he was loved and he didn't need to seek affection in compromising ways that were wrong. Thus, he was able "day after day" to brush off the advances of Potiphar's wife.

On the other hand, Jacob loved Joseph more than his

other sons, and one wonders about Joseph's lack of tact—and maybe a bit of arrogance—in telling his brothers about his dreams stating pretty unsubtly that HE was his father's favorite.

Joseph also demonstrated cleverness in negotiating. He didn't reveal himself to his brothers immediately and he tested their words for truth (Gen. 42:16). Yet, on the other hand, Joseph's policy led to feudalism. He used the famine to buy up all the land of Egypt for Pharaoh in exchange for providing the people with food from Pharaoh's granaries.

David

The Bible devotes nearly sixty chapters to David (1 Sam. 16–1 King 2 and 1 Chron. 11–29), which is more than any other individual in Scripture commands except Jesus. David was the world's most famous king, handsome, charismatic, gifted. "The sweet psalmist of Israel," the Bible calls him (2 Sam 23:1). He played the harp with such exquisite skill that he was able to coax Saul out of his bad moods. The Bible says David was "handsome" (1 Sam. 16:18 NASV). The women sang, "Saul has slain his thousands, and David his ten thousands" (1 Sam. 18:7). He married the king's daughter. He was a tremendous warrior, both as a foot soldier and a commander, and as a monarch he "executed judgment and justice" (2 Sam. 8:15 KJV). He was the model of Christ. I named my son after him.

I don't want to write merely about David's glory but also about his crises, and he had more than his share. Mention David's crises, and his affair with Bathsheba immediately leaps into our minds. I have stood several times in the old City of David in Jerusalem, which is built on the slopes of those Judean hills, and thought how easy it would have been for David to stand on his roof terrace and casually look over and gaze at Bathsheba bathing after a hot Jerusalem day.

And this was not David's only sin. His warlike foreign policy was so bloody that God would not permit him to build the temple, the ambition of his heart. As if to nail down the point, the Bible says this twice. When David became king he immediately got involved in a series of campaigns to shore up Israel's boundaries—against the Philistines on the southwest (near what is now Tel Aviv), the Ammonites (who were located in what is now Amman, the capital of Jordan), and the Syrians, who to this day are one of Israel's major adversaries. God gave him victory wherever he went (2 Sam. 8:6, 14 and 1 Chron. 18:13). But it was bloody, far too bloody for God's taste. "You have shed much blood and have waged great wars; you shall not build a house to my name, because you have shed so much blood" (1 Chron. 22:8). It appears from the chronology that God was more willing to forgive David's lust for Bathsheba than his lust for war. So David's son Solomon built the temple.

There was something worse, in my view, because it was so despicable. David's closest aide was a man named Joab. They spent many years together. Joab did a lot of David's dirty work. He was the one David assigned to order Bathsheba's husband into combat. He was the one who assassinated Absalom, after Absalom attempted a coup d'état. I can almost hear Joab say, "Never mind whether it's right, I'm doing it for the king." The variation on that in modern life: "Never mind whether it's right; the boss told me to do it." Joab sacrificed everything for his leader. And what thanks did he get? At the very last David got miffed at Joab. Some of the last words David spoke before dying were to tell Solomon, "Do not let his gray head go down to the grave in peace" (1 Kings 2:6

NIV). One of Solomon's first acts as king was to order Joab assassinated. That done, Solomon prayed for a "wise and an understanding heart" (1 Kings 3:9 KJV).

Given this kind of deeply flawed record, why was David so loved of God? Why was he praised for doing right in the eyes of the Lord except in the matter of Uriah? Why was he more renowned than any king of Israel, before or since? Much of the answer, of course, is that David repented and was contrite. But part of the answer also must lie in his execution of justice over all the people. David's own words reveal, despite his lapses, a fundamental commitment to justice:

> For the needy shall not always be forgotten,
> And the hope of the poor shall not perish forever. [Ps. 9:18]

> For the word of the LORD is upright;
> And all his work is done in faithfulness.
> He loves righteousness and justice;
> The earth is full of the mercy of the LORD.
> [Ps. 33: 4–5]

David, like many of us, had a divided nature. He was a man who spoke eloquently of justice and truth and peace, yet a man given to war. He was a man who also fought an interior war, who was the sweet psalmist of Israel, the precursor of Christ, but who would order his closest, most intimate aide assassinated. He was a man who got so involved in an affair that he was willing to commit murder to cover his tracks.

Often a crisis has the effect of putting what is ultimately important in sharp relief. We are told that drowning persons see replays of their entire lives in those last few moments. Often a crisis reveals to us who we really are, which we may have known or suspected all along.

As I have insisted throughout this book, we are most

vulnerable in our areas of strength. David was tempted by Bathsheba not because he was the hunchback of Notre Dame but because women responded to him. He, too, had heard the women's songs, celebrating his military victories as they danced before him. And those tunes probably still rang in his ear. David knew he was handsome. People tend not to acknowledge a problem until they get caught, and David did not immediately face up to his sin with Bathsheba. The prophet Nathan had to go to David and tell him a pointed story: A rich man with many flocks and herds took a poor man's only lamb to serve at a meal. David was furious over the story—a bit of righteous indignation—until Nathan said to him, "You are the man" (2 Sam. 12:7). Then, having been caught, David turned contrite, and out of that experience he wrote Psalm 51, one of the most poignant and powerful poems about repentance in all literature. At least he ultimately faced up to what he had done. In Psalm 32:3 David tells us graphically what happens when we refuse to face up to our wrongdoing: "When I declared not my sin, my body wasted away through my groaning all day long, For day and night thy hand was heavy upon me; my strength was dried up as by the heat of summer." We do not have a good psychological understanding as to why denial of our problems is so debilitating, but it is. Ask David.

In Psalm 51 David pointed out this truth: Real joy and gladness and delight did not flow out of his affair with the beautiful Bathsheba. As a matter of fact, his affair with Bathsheba hung over David constantly, like a pall. Rather, real joy and gladness and pleasure and delight flowed out of David's *repentance*.

What are we to make of our crises, then? Of David and how he handled his crises? My good friend, Carlisle Dunaway, an attorney, has an interesting approach to characters of the Bible. He feels more sympathetic to Cain than to Abel, to Ishmael than Isaac, to Esau than Jacob, to the elder brother in the story of the prodigal son, to Martha than Mary. He feels that often the person who has been responsible, who did his or her duty, who didn't go off, such as the elder brother or Martha, fares much less satisfactorily, even in God's eyes, than the person who makes egregious mistakes and repents, as did David, the beloved of God. This is a knotty biblical paradox.

But if there is something to be derived from this paradox, it could be this: If God only blessed those who lived impeccably and flawlessly, crisis free, where would the model be for the rest of us? In Jacob, in the younger brother, in David, we see our own flaws. And when we see how they repented, how they were blessed, then we have guidelines to handle crises. Better yet, we have hope that we will, with God's help, conquer crises and emerge newly energized, with greater power to be the servants God wants us to be.

Conclusion

It is my intention that this book provide hope—that *all* of us, big and small, meek and mighty, may realize that we have power. We are not powerless. Each one of us has talents and skills. The delight of this discovery can shore up our sense of worth. It can enable us to live in the paradox of effectiveness and joy.

But it is also my intention that this book provide an admonition. Our use of power, indeed, even our feeling of power, can quickly thrust us into situations of peril where we use it for ill, perhaps unwittingly at first, then deliberately, finally blatantly.

In the Persian Gulf war, the United States learned that sometimes it is easier to use power as a weapon of war than later as the olive branch of peace. This is true for us as individuals, too. It is easier to use our power to tear down than it is to restore.

Ultimately, of course, we as a nation, we as brothers and sisters in community, and we as individuals must decide how we will use our power. The Scriptures of our frontispiece lay out the options: In Job, the crafty and wily hand of the mighty was being used against the needy. But Moses' hand of the mighty prevailed in triumph against the oppressor Egypt.

One choice leads to blessing and the other choice toward cursing. Choose blessing and choose life.

General Index

Index of Scripture References

Old Testament

Genesis
1:26—41
14:18-20—40
18:19—37
37-50—147
37:4—148
39:3—148
39:6—147
39:9—148
41:16—148
42:16—149
49:3—41
50:19—148
50:20—148

Exodus
1:14—35
4:10—135
5-12—28
9:16—33, 34, 35
15:6—35
18:18—120
21:2—38
21:24—67
22:3—106
32:1—35

Leviticus
19:9-10—38

Numbers
14:13—35

Deuteronomy
4:37—35
16:18—38, 100
34:10-12—6

Joshua
16:10—35
17:13—35

Judges
1:28-35—35
11:12—28, 36
14:19—72
16—41

1 Samuel
2:1-10—35
2:9—38
8:1-7—38
16:18—149
18:7—149
28:20, 22—41

2 Samuel
8:6—150
8:14—150
8:15—38, 149
12:7—152
20:24—35
23:1—149

1 Kings
2:6—150
3:9—151
5:13-14—35
9:15—35
9:22—35
10:9—39
19:6, 8—41

1 Chronicles
18:13—150
18:14—38
22:8—150
29:11—33

2 Chronicles
8:3—36
8:8—35
9:8—39
17:10—28
20:6—34

161

Index of Biblical Names